100

Classic Toys

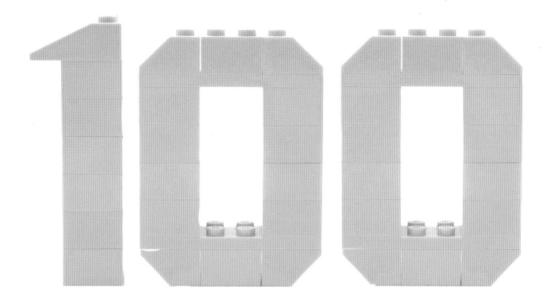

Classic Toys

DAVID SMITH

VIVAYS PUBLISHING

Published by Vivays Publishing
www.vivays-publishing.com

A catalogue record for this book is available from the British Library

ISBN 978-1-908126-05-4

Publishing Director: Lee Ripley
Design: Price Watkins

Printed in China

CONTENTS

INTRODUCTION

Not all toys are created equal. Although every toy enters the world full of hope, most quietly disappear after a few years.

This book is dedicated to those toys that have beaten the odds and established themselves as the hardy perennials of the industry. Loved by generations, they have a timeless appeal that keeps kids coming back for more.

For some, this is down to the perfect simplicity of their design. For others it is the imaginative world they offer a doorway into. Some of these toys were once lost, but have recently been relaunched. Others have been with us continuously for decades, centuries or even millennia.

Our criteria for judging the toys were simple. In order to be included, a toy must have proved its long-term appeal and still be readily available. This inevitably meant that many all-time greats were not included (will someone please relaunch Sky Battle?), simply because they aren't on sale any more – so if your favourite childhood toy isn't included, this is probably why, and I apologise.

One of the benefits of writing this book, of course, is that most of *my* favourite childhood toys are here. Action Man, toy soldiers, trains, cars – this is standard issue stuff for boys. The first toy I can remember was a Massey Ferguson tractor from Reindeer Toys, a South African company, I believe. I've still got it (although time and play have converted it to a three-wheeler) and it now lives in my boys' toy box, which is where all old toys should be, bringing enjoyment to a new generation.

The choice available to youngsters today has expanded dramatically, and licensing now plays a big part in determining which toys are going to succeed and which will struggle. Having a major film or TV series behind a range of toys gives it a huge advantage, but it's interesting that so many of the toys covered in these pages, although many have been given a licensing brush-up in recent years, originally launched without that safety net.

Toys and games like Connect 4, Operation and Twister may have big friends alongside them now,

in the form of licensed versions featuring *Toy Story*, *The Simpsons* and *High School Musical*, but the first time they ventured into the playground, they ventured alone, which makes their longevity all the more impressive, I think.

But while looking back is fun (and it is sadly true that not all relaunches capture the full glory of the original toy), I don't want to give the impression that new toys aren't exciting as well. At the end of this book we've included a few of the newer toys that we think have a good chance of becoming the classic toys of tomorrow, but it's never easy to predict the future (even the Magic 8 Ball couldn't help us here).

Certainly in the coming years there will be more new toys clamouring for attention and more relaunches to spark a debate on which is better: the original or the new version.

Hopefully you will remember many of the toys in these pages. Hopefully you played with many of them as a child. Hopefully your children or grandchildren are playing with some of them today.

Because that's the whole point of this book.

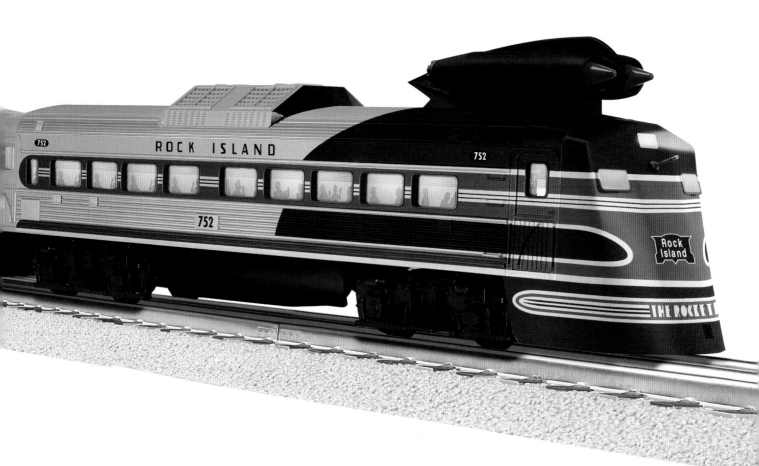

1 Building toys

ALPHABET BLOCKS
MECCANO/ERECTOR SET
LINCOLN LOGS
TINKERTOY
LEGO
STOKYS
KAPLA
STICKLE BRICKS

ALPHABET BLOCKS

www.unclegoose.com

Simple wooden blocks have been used as playthings for centuries, but in 1693, the English philosopher John Locke suggested that adding the letters of the alphabet to these blocks would turn them into a valuable educational toy.

The truth is that wooden blocks were educational long before anything was painted on them. Early home-made blocks imparted lessons on spatial awareness, physics and cooperation (wooden blocks are often the first toy that children share with siblings or friends), developing hand-eye coordination and problem-solving skills.

The development of wooden blocks accelerated in the 19th century when the German teacher, soldier and museum curator Friedrich Froebel invented the concept of the kindergarten (he came up with the name as well, clever chap that) and designed a range of coloured wooden blocks (which he called 'gifts') to use in them.

Alphabet blocks are now a staple of nursery schools and play chests around the world, manufactured by countless companies, including Uncle Goose , Schylling and John Crane.

It was Froebel who also came up with the idea of 'free play', unstructured time where a child is allowed to simply play, with no agenda or goal. This is a philosophy perfectly suited to the use of wooden blocks, where children can experiment, explore and discover.

Alphabet blocks were inducted into America's National Toy Hall of Fame in 2003. What took them so long?

MECCANO/ERECTOR SET

1901
Inventor: Frank Hornby
www.meccano.com

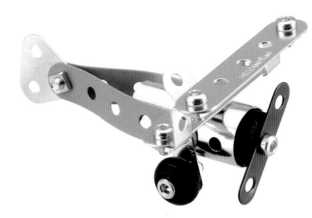

Keeping the kids occupied is a challenge familiar to all parents, but not many have done such a successful job of it as Frank Hornby. Working with metal plates, screws and nuts, Hornby developed a construction system to entertain his children that he would patent in 1901 as 'Mechanics Made Easy'. We know it better as *Meccano*, as the toy (after a few modifications) became known in 1907.

Not only were Hornby's children impressed, thousands of others were as well and the first *Meccano* factory opened in Liverpool in 1907.

Although the brand has changed ownership many times and sets have been modified over the years to include electric motors, plastic pieces and various colour schemes, two key things have remained constant with the metal sets — the half-inch spacing of the perforations on the *Meccano* pieces and the 5/32-inch Whitworth thread on the nuts and bolts. The result is that pieces from the earliest sets can still be incorporated into modern *Meccano* constructions.

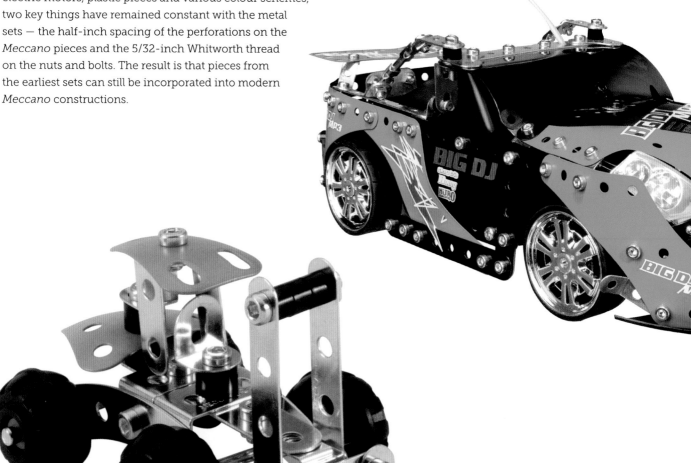

From its red-and-green heyday to the high-tech sets of today, *Meccano* has retained an educational element. Rumours of deliberate errors being inserted into instruction manuals to test a child's mental dexterity are officially denied (but what a great excuse for a mistake, 'Yeah, I did that on purpose... to test the kids'), but the constructions are often testing enough without any errors, deliberate or otherwise.

The famed 'Outfit No. 10', for example, included instructions for building a dumper truck, an automatic gantry crane, a double-decker bus, a 4-4-0 passenger locomotive, a beam bridge, a railway service crane, a block-setting crane, a sports motor car, a coal tipper, a cargo ship, a lifting shovel and an automatic snow loader. Now there's a challenge.

Meccano is distributed in the United States under the Erector brand name. Erector sets, invented by A. C. Gilbert in 1913, were similar to Meccano in many ways and were the construction system of choice for American children until waning interest led to the collapse of the company in 1967.

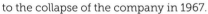

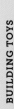

LINCOLN LOGS

1916
Inventor: John Lloyd Wright
http://lincolnlogs.knex.com

John Lloyd Wright's famous father, the architect Frank Lloyd Wright, must take at least some of the credit for the invention of *Lincoln Logs*. Frank, who had played with the wooden 'gifts' of Friedrich Froebel (see Alphabet Blocks, page 10) as a child, designed an earthquake-resistant hotel in Japan and it was while watching the construction process that his son John had an idea for an interlocking wooden construction toy.

The invention of *Lincoln Logs* was perfectly timed to tap into the growing legend of the American frontier, receding into memory but still a potent symbol of American independence and hardiness at a time when the world was changing rapidly, and not always for the better. Basing his design on the classic frontier log cabin, Wright created a toy that harkened back to an earlier, simpler way of life that many Americans yearned for.

America's special relationship with the log cabin (many Presidential candidates in the 19th century insisted they had been born in a log cabin in an attempt to connect with the voters) made *Lincoln Logs* an almost guaranteed success – no doubt some of the first parents to buy a box for their children would have been born in log cabins themselves (unlike most of those Presidential candidates).

Although it has faded over the years, the magic of that period in American history has never really gone away, making *Lincoln Logs* an enduring symbol of the frontier spirit.

TINKERTOY

1914
Inventor: Charles Pajeau
www.hasbro.com

Some toys take endless refinement and development before they are ready to be unveiled. Others are just sitting there waiting to be discovered. *Tinkertoy* fits firmly into the latter category.

Stone mason and designer Charles Pajeau saw a group of children playing with cotton reels, pencils and sticks, poking the pencils and sticks in the holes in the reels. This looked like a toy to Pajeau and, with just a few adjustments (*Tinkertoy* did not require much tinkering), the new toy was patented in 1913 and launched the following year.

The major addition to the basic concept was the provision of eight further holes around the edge of the circular wooden pieces that act as the hubs in any *Tinkertoy* construction. Allowing for connecting rods to be added in a range of positions offered tremendous flexibility in construction and the result was a toy that young minds found, and still find, engrossing.

The educational benefits of *Tinkertoy* are a welcome by-product of the toy's design, but its true strength lies in the endless possibilities offered by those few, simple pieces. One combination, designed by students at MIT, is even capable of playing a mean game of noughts and crosses.

Most children will settle for less ambitious projects, but the fact that it's possible to build a working computer out of these wooden (now plastic) pieces proves that whatever a child dreams up, *Tinkertoy* will be up to the challenge.

Vintage *Tinkertoy* sets.

LEGO

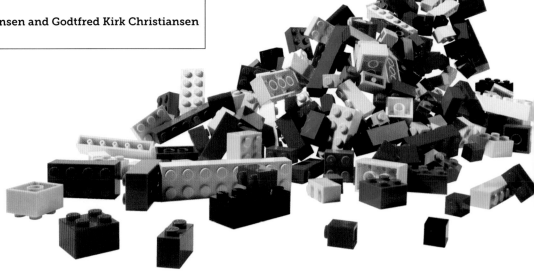

1955
Inventors: Ole Kirk Christiansen and Godtfred Kirk Christiansen
www.lego.com

*L*EGO had been trading successfully as a toy company for over 20 years, with a variety of wooden toys (including a very successful mallard duck), building blocks and even familiar-looking hollow plastic bricks, when Godtfred Kirk Christiansen got to thinking about a new type of toy – a play 'system' where every product in the range could combine with the others to create bigger and more ambitious worlds for children to lose themselves in.

In 1955, the *LEGO* System was launched, using a revised version of the earlier brick. *LEGO* bricks could now grip each other firmly, yet remained easy to disassemble. The Town Plan range was at the heart

of the new system, comprising 28 construction sets and eight vehicles.

Today, around 19 billion *LEGO* bricks are produced each year, but the most important thing is how the bricks can fit together – a set of six eight-stud *LEGO* bricks can combine in 915,103,765 different ways (and we've verified each one), giving amazing flexibility when it comes to construction.

LEGO quickly expanded into different themes, offering castles, spaceships, pirate ships and cities. To populate this new landscape, the minifigure appeared in 1978

and has gone on to become one of the most popular and collectible elements of the *LEGO* world.

The *LEGO* System continues to grow at an amazing rate, with new themes added every year. Popular movie tie-ins, such as *Star Wars* and Harry Potter sets, rub shoulders with entirely original creations like Kingdoms, Atlantis and Pharoah's Quest.

The *LEGO* story shows no signs of ending anytime soon.

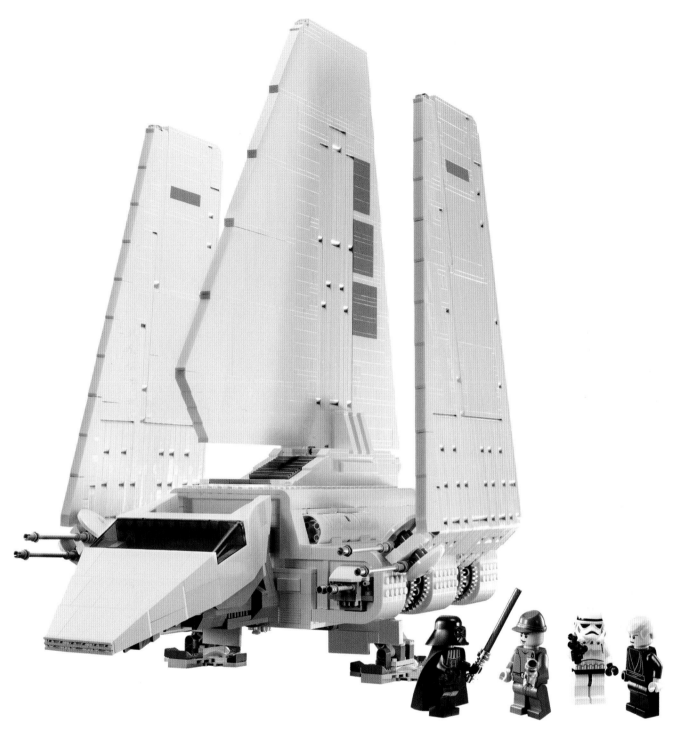

STOKYS

1942
Inventor: Max and Arnold Stokmann
www.stokys.ch

There are many advantages to remaining neutral during a war, but there are one or two disadvantages as well. As the Second World War raged, the Swiss found it impossible to buy their children toys like *Meccano*, with production of metal toys being severely curtailed or halted altogether in combatant countries.

Swiss brothers Max and Arnold Stokmann decided to do something about this and developed a Meccano-like construction system of their own, *Stokys*, which launched in 1942.

Originally, *Stokys* used a 10 mm metric hole spacing, but the Stockmann brothers were advised to adopt the half-inch pattern of the established *Meccano* brand. With pieces made from lightweight aluminium and the benefits of Swiss precision-engineering techniques, *Stokys* established itself as a firm favourite with Swiss children.

The brand suffered under pressure from new plastic-based toys, and by the turn of the millennium it was largely confined to hobbyists and adult enthusiasts, before a group of those enthusiasts bought the company and relaunched it in 2008.

Stokys sets, in the familiar yellow boxes, are now pleasing a new generation of children, in Switzerland and around the world.

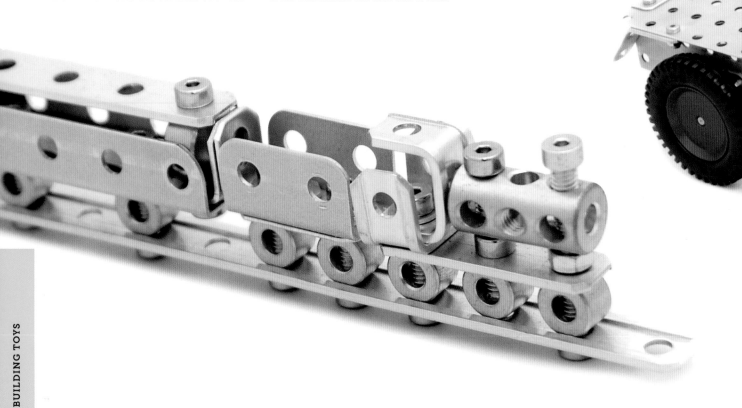

KAPLA

1988
Inventor: Tom van der Bruggen
www.kapla.com

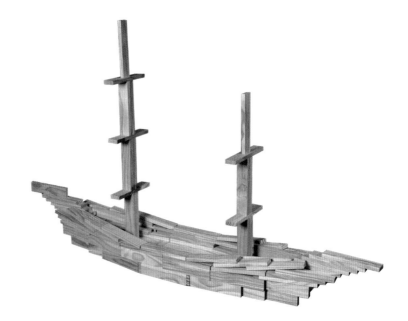

It's safe to say that Tom van der Bruggen has an active imagination. As a 25-year-old furniture-restorer, it takes imagination to sell a successful business and pursue your dream. It takes even more imagination for that dream to involve building a castle in France.

The Dutchman found his castle amid the ruins of a French farmhouse in 1988 and set about developing his plans with the aid of small wooden blocks. The blocks proved unsatisfactory, so van der Bruggen developed a new block, based on the ratio 1:3:5 — one unit of thickness, three times that for width and five times the width for the length.

The *KAPLA* plank was the result, an abbreviation of 'Kabouter Plankjes', which means 'gnome planks' – which is a name we think could have worked. The wooden pieces are perfectly proportioned to make structures as simple or as complex as the user desires.

Surprisingly, it is the uniformity of the planks in the *KAPLA* system that adds complexity. A variety of sizes and shapes might seem to offer more potential, but by solving the problems inherent in using pieces of the same size, the *KAPLA* planks foster greater concentration and help to develop spatial awareness.

There is even evidence that playing with *KAPLA* in a group environment helps children with communication problems and these little wooden planks are part of the French national educational curriculum.

KAPLA planks are now sold all over the world, but there is one more poignant detail about this success story. To finance the launch of his new dream, Van der Bruggen had to wave goodbye to his old one. He sold his French 'castle' to raise the funds.

STICKLE BRICKS

1968
Inventor: Denys Fisher
www.sticklebricks.org.uk

When most children are too ill to go to school, they may lie in bed reading comics or watching TV. Not Denys Fisher. The Leeds schoolboy tackled weightier matters when he was confined to bed for six weeks by illness – reading *Lamb's Infinitesimal Calculus*.

It's lucky for us that he did because (a) now we don't have to, and (b) the love of mathematics that developed in those six weeks spurred Fisher on to launch his own engineering company in 1960, and from that sprang Denys Fisher Toys – with his most notable inventions being the *Spirograph* (see page 192) and *Stickle Bricks*.

Stickle Bricks is a construction toy with a difference. Aimed at the very young, it comes in big blocks that even little hands can fit together quite easily. 'An easy way to build big toys!' claimed the slogan on early boxes, and those boxes were right.

The inclusion of various shapes, accessories like axles and wheels, and the bold colours catch the eye of toddlers and reward their interest with instant results. Stick two pieces together and they're instantly hooked, reaching for another piece to add to their creation.

Having spent years trying to perfect the *Spirograph*, Fisher apparently dreamed up *Stickle Bricks* with no trouble at all. Which is probably why they are so wonderful.

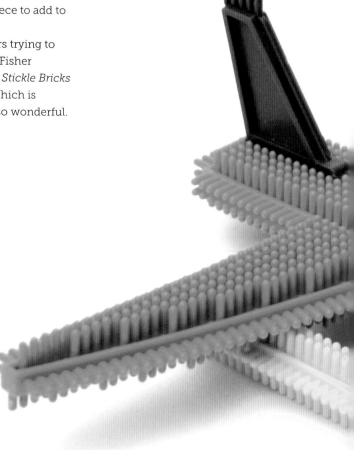

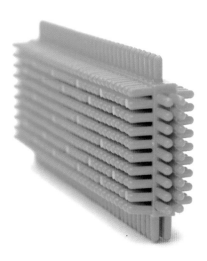

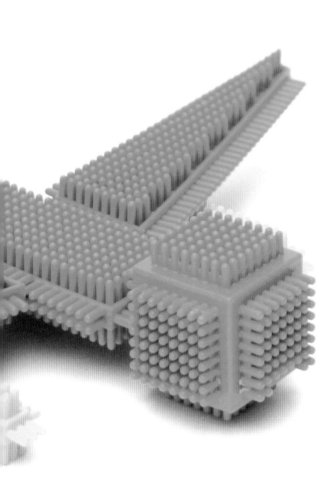

2 Games and puzzles

BUCKAROO!
CONNECT FOUR
TWISTER
ELECTRIC FOOTBALL
GUESS WHO?
MAGIC 8 BALL
HUNGRY HUNGRY HIPPOS
REBOUND
JACK-IN-THE-BOX
KERPLUNK
BARREL OF MONKEYS
RUBIK'S CUBE
JACKS
JENGA
MOUSE TRAP
MARBLES
BATTLESHIP
ROCK 'EM SOCK 'EM ROBOTS
LABYRINTH
SUBBUTEO
JIGSAW PUZZLES
OPERATION
MASTERMIND
TIDDLYWINKS

BUCKAROO!

1970
Inventor: Julius Cooper
www.hasbro.com

Poor Buckaroo. Derided as a bad-tempered mule ('he's as moody as all get-out!' as the rules gleefully inform us), he is really only demanding fair treatment from his owners. Consider what he has to put up with. Players take turns to load a ridiculous number of objects onto his back. Some of them (canteen, bedroll, shovel, rope) are perfectly reasonable and necessary for any prospecting expedition.

But should he really be expected to carry a cowboy hat? Couldn't the cowboy wear that? And what about the guitar? Carrying it is only half the problem – what about when someone tries to play it round the campfire, and perhaps sing?

And frankly, expecting him to carry a stick of dynamite, which is notoriously unstable, is just cruel. So the mule inevitably objects, bucking everything off his back and reducing all the players to laughter. Then they start loading him up again.

Buckaroo! (not as posh as the original, having lost its hyphenated name somewhere along the way) gradually builds suspense as each item is loaded on. Different sensitivity settings in the modern version mean the mule can be as ornery as you like and the tension can become exquisite as you try to balance a big object on an already overloaded saddle.

The same principle was used (with less success) in a *Jaws* game, but *Buckaroo!* saw off that competition and has appeared under various guises, including a cameo as a camel in an Ali Babar version, and as Woody's faithful steed Bullseye in a *Toy Story* spin-off.

1970 *Buck-a-roo!*, by Ideal.

CONNECT FOUR

1974
Inventor: Howard Wexler
www.hasbro.com

Invented by Howard Wexler (and not, as the popular urban legend has it, David Bowie), *Connect Four* is basically an expanded version of noughts and crosses, only now you have to get four of your pieces in line on an expanded playing area.

The tactile nature of the counters and the sound each piece makes as it is dropped into place makes this a surprisingly satisfying game to play, and the level of thought needed to plot your way to victory is fitting for a game invented by a man with a Ph.D. in psychology.

It is actually possible to guarantee victory in *Connect Four* as long as you start first – although thankfully not many people realise this and we're certainly not going to spoil things by explaining how to win here.

The game is inevitably complicated as pieces go missing over the years, and you may eventually find yourself having to plot a lightning victory to compensate for only having six counters at your disposal, but that just adds to the challenge.

Connect Four is one of those games that, periodically, is revamped and relaunched with new features, but the classic original version remains the best and the concept is so pure it really doesn't need dressing up. Just hang on to those counters.

TWISTER

1966
Inventors: Charles F. Foley and Neil Rabens
www.hasbro.com

W ho hasn't played *Twister* as a child at a birthday party? For that matter, who hasn't played it as a teenager, hoping to get into a compromising position with a certain member of the opposite sex? *Twister* was actually seen as controversial in the swinging sixties, denounced as 'sex in a box' by individuals who obviously had a very shaky understanding of sex.

The executives at Milton Bradley were concerned that the game might attract such criticism when they launched it in 1966, but its success was assured when legendary TV host Johnny Carson and actress Eva Gabor got entangled on a *Twister* mat during an episode of the *Tonight* show. Helped by that appearance, *Twister* sold three million copies in its first year.

The controversy appears risible now. *Twister* is a great ice-breaker and it is impossible not to crack a smile as the little spinner dictates which hand or foot goes where on the plastic mat, before gravity has its way and someone loses their balance. It also raises an interesting etiquette question regarding socks. Wear them (and risk slipping on the plastic mat at a crucial point), or take them off?

The four colours on the mat have also led to criticism from those who feel that colour-blind players are excluded from the fun. Does everyone want to have a pop at this classic game?

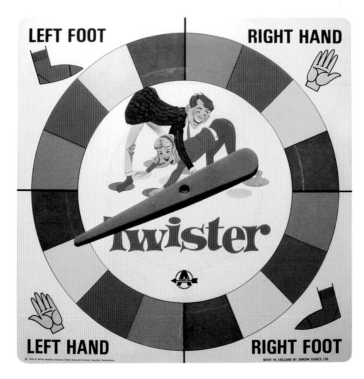

1966 *Twister*, by Arrow Games.

RIGHT FOOT

The game that ties you up in knots!

Twister

Kids

AGE 6+ | 10 | 2+ PLAYERS   ADULT ASSEMBLY REQUIRED

ELECTRIC FOOTBALL

1947
Inventor: Norman Sas
www.miggle.com

Triple threat quarterback
from 1986 UK version.

Electric Football has been beguiling young football fans for over 70 years – yet Bill Bryson, in *The Life and Times of the Thunderbolt Kid*, called it "possibly the worst toy ever built". How can these two facts be reconciled?

It is common to see dismissive reviews of *Electric Football*, bemoaning the fact that the players move fairly randomly and individual plays never really unfold as drawn up on the chalkboard, but this is missing the most important element. The game is, simply, fun.

What American football fan wouldn't want the chance to take their favourite team into battle with an arch rival, lining the players up on a realistic, fully marked football field, choosing the formations and plays that they think will lead to success and then sitting back while the whole thing magically comes to life and the players start to move, however randomly?

People have been unable to resist this sales pitch for decades. Companies including Tudor, Gotham and Coleco have produced a variety of sets with different sized, electrically agitated playing fields. So what if the players are often agitated in the wrong direction (a problem in any sport, but especially American football)?

Despite pressure from videogames where the players actually go where they are told, *Electric Football* remains a cult toy and leagues exist around the world, with grown-ups enjoying the action as much as kids.

Electric Football might not always work, but it's fun giving it the old college try...

1986 UK version, by
Peter Pan Playthings.

1986 UK version.

GUESS WHO?

1979
Inventors: Ora and Theo Coster
www.hasbro.com

Guess Who? is the finest creation of the Israeli couple, Ora and Theo Coster, whose company (now called Theora Design) has dreamed up over 155 toy and game concepts that have been licensed by various companies.

The original *Guess Who?* is based on the faces of 24 cartoon characters – a mixture of men and women with distinguishing characteristics, including hair colour, glasses and hats. Each player picks a card representing one of the characters and must then attempt to guess which card their opponent is holding by asking questions. Does your person have blonde hair? Do they wear glasses? Do they have blue eyes?

A certain amount of luck plays its part – a question can lead to just a few characters being eliminated, or the majority of them – and the pressure as your opponent closes in can lead to some desperate guesses in an attempt to snatch a victory.

Some players will inevitably try to get clever, combining different elements into questions that can guarantee to eliminate half the remaining characters (you'll have to decide if such combination questions are allowed or not), and quixotic types might simply attempt to guess the character outright, turning the game into a sort of Russian roulette, where any turn might be your last. Thankfully, these people will nearly always lose.

MAGIC 8 BALL

1950
Inventors: Albert Carter and Abe Bookman
www.mattel.com

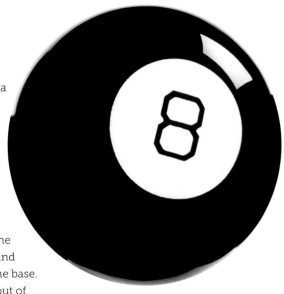

*T*he *Magic 8 Ball* has its origins at least partly in a promotional stunt (see also *Airfix*, page 184). Alabe Crafts – a play on the Christian names of the two partners – had been producing the 'Syco-Slate' fortune-telling toy for some time when Bookman had the idea of encasing it in a 'crystal ball', the perfect setting for such a gadget.

In *Timeless Toys*, Tim Walsh explains how a billiards company saw this new version and, in 1950, asked if Alabe could make one in the form of a black billiard ball as a promotional device. Bookman liked the finished product so much he decided to stick with it and the *Magic 8 Ball* was released to the public.

Despite attracting some criticism from people who believed the *Magic 8 Ball* was a way to commune with evil spirits, most people took a saner view

of what was, after all, just a bit of harmless fun. The toy houses a 20-sided polygon adrift in a sea of thick liquid. When the *Magic 8 Ball* is stood up on its flat end, the polygon disappears into the murky depths.

Ask a yes-or-no question (there are all sorts of rituals involved in how you should properly pose your question to the all-knowing 8 Ball), turn it over and look at the viewing window in the base. The polygon will slowly appear out of the gloom and present you with your answer.

Understanding human nature, the inventors of the *Magic 8 Ball* decided to offer 10 positive responses alongside five negatives and five non-committals. If only parents offered a similar ratio in their responses, right kids?

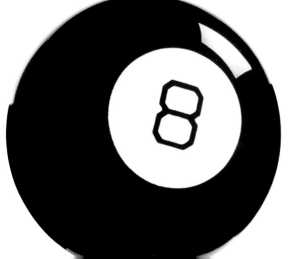

HUNGRY HUNGRY HIPPOS

1978
www.hasbro.com

Anyone knows that a hungry hippo is not an animal to be trifled with. But a *hungry* hungry hippo, well that's a problem on an entirely different scale. Such a beast might selfishly gobble down anything it could find, regardless of how many other hippos happened to be hungry at the same time.

In *Hungry Hungry Hippos* (interestingly enough, this was originally known as *Hungry Hippos* in the UK, perhaps they'd eaten earlier), there are four ravenous hippos, each intent only on scoffing down as many marbles as it can. The four contestants face off around a feeding area, into which an appetising (to a hungry hippo) selection of marbles is released. By slamming down on the tail of a hippo, players can make their beast stretch out its neck and take a bite at the marbles. Sometimes the hippo will be lucky and grab one or two marbles, sometimes it will merely nudge a marble towards an opponent.

In the ensuing chaos, one hippo should emerge as the winner. And then it's time to play again, because these hippos get hungry again in a heartbeat.

Hungry Hungry Hippos taps cleverly into the intrinsic appeal of the hippopotamus. Despite being extremely dangerous creatures in the wild, we just can't take them seriously and the frantic action of *Hungry Hungry Hippos* (once celebrated in the satirical UK puppet show *Spitting Image*, in a sketch where Prince Charles played the game with evident delight) makes it irresistible to children, adults and princes alike.

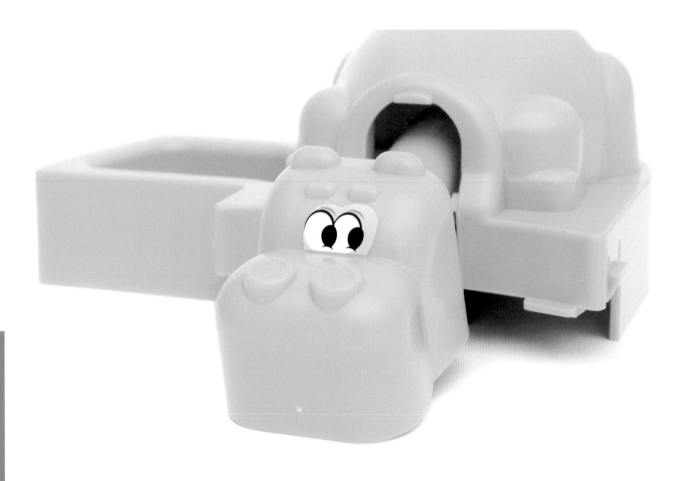

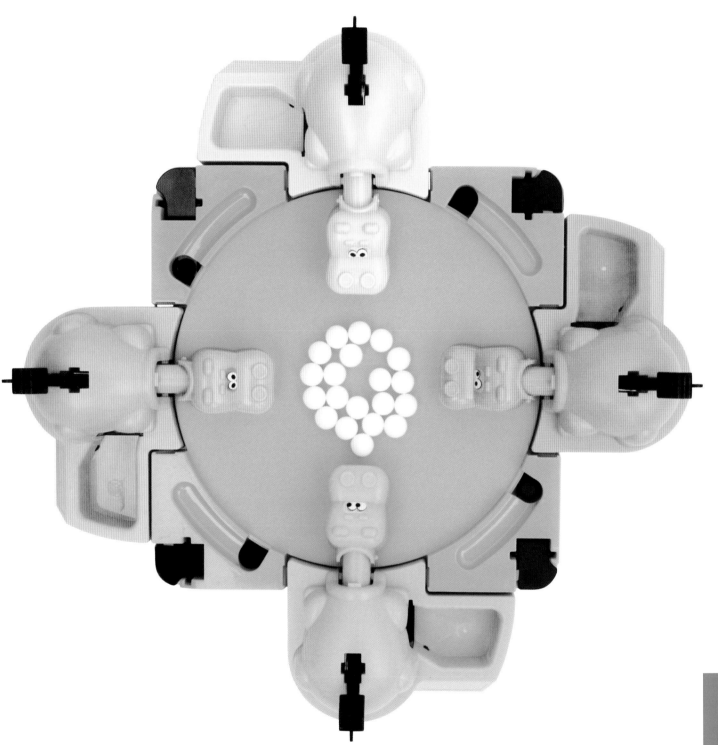

REBOUND

1971
www.mattel.com

*R*ebound is a derivative of the table shuffleboard game, where players attempt to slide pucks into a scoring zone and outscore their opponents. *Rebound* (or *Two Cushion Rebound Game* to give it its full name) works on the same principle on a much smaller board, buts adds two rubber bands for extra fun (adding rubber bands always increases enjoyment – it's a basic principle of toy design).

Each player or team has four colour-coded 'pucks' (ball-bearings encased in plastic, just like the one used in the late-lamented *Crossfire* game). Sliding the pucks down the board causes them to rebound off the rubber bands and come to rest on the other side, hopefully scattering your opponents' pucks and finishing up in the highest-scoring zone.

Get things wrong, of course, and your puck will either fall impotently short of its target, or career wildly into the 'pit' and score nothing at all. Worst of all, it might bump into one of your own pucks and knock that out of a scoring position as well. Clearly, there is much to master in *Rebound*.

There's something endearingly old-fashioned about the game, with its echoes of pub pastimes like shove ha'penny, which made it feel somewhat retro even when it first launched.

Rebound is now marketed by Mattel, although a *Two Cushion Bumpershot* game is produced under the Ideal label by Poof Slinky.

1980 *Rebound*, by Ideal.

JACK-IN-THE-BOX

The *Jack-in-the-box* plays on a child's endless desire to be surprised – scared in a fun way. A handle on the side of the box plays a familiar tune when wound ('Pop Goes the Weasel' is the traditional choice) and then the top of the box pops open and 'Jack' springs out.

Aside from Jack himself, one other thing jumps out when considering this classic toy – it isn't really that surprising. After a couple of goes a child will know what's coming, but there's delicious anticipation in trying to guess when Jack will make his appearance.

By turning the handle very slowly, moreover, a child can enjoy a feeling of control as the big moment arrives (and you can even hear the interior mechanism clicking into life as the vital note approaches).

The concept is believed to date back to the 13th century, but it remains a staple ingredient in toy chests today thanks to a concerted campaign of diversification. Early examples housed a leering devil inside the box (it's a miracle it ever caught on), but today the aim is to entertain rather than terrify and *Jack-in-the-boxes* are now produced in a vast selection of characters, with an equally wide range of musical accompaniments.

KERPLUNK

1967
Inventors: Eddy Goldfarb and Rene Soriano
www.mattel.com

*K*erplunk could hardly fail. Not only does it have one of the best names a toy has ever been blessed with, it also incorporates another classic toy, the humble marble (see page 54). In *Kerplunk*, players take it in turns to remove plastic sticks from the criss-crossing centre section of a plastic tube, hoping not to trigger an avalanche of marbles, which are balanced precariously on top of the sticks. The winner is the player who, at the end of the game, has unseated the fewest marbles.

Kerplunk assailed us with an irresistible barrage of selling points — the name, the beautiful box, the impressive appearance of the toy when set up, the instant understanding of the basic gameplay. Anyone who wasn't

paying attention would soon come running when the first marbles started to fall, unleashing an unholy racket that was guaranteed to raise a smile and catch attention.

The unpredictability of the game only adds to the enjoyment. You may think you are safely removing an insignificant stick, only to watch in horror as a clutch of marbles finds its way to the bottom of the tube. You may sweat as you delicately ease out a seemingly critical section, only to break into a smile of relief as the endangered marbles cling to each other like trapeze artists and remain aloft.

You never really master *Kerplunk*, but it's so much fun, you don't really care.

1967 *Kerplunk*, by Ideal.

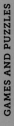

BARREL OF MONKEYS

1966
Inventor: Leonard Marks
www.hasbro.com

One of the best-named children's toys may have had a much drabber title if not for the fact that 'Barrel of Fun' was already in use by another company when the creative types at Lakeside Toys were tweaking the design of a new game.

Using s-shaped hooks, the proposed game involved picking up one hook with another and then continuing to add as many hooks as possible to the chain before it broke.

Keen on the concept, but forced to think of a new name, Lakeside benefitted from a stroke of genius when the phrase 'more fun than a barrel of monkeys' popped into someone's head. A quick re-design of the s-shaped hooks (and a switch from wire to plastic) and the classic *Barrel of Monkeys* game was ready to launch in 1966.

There were originally 12 monkeys in three colours (four each of red, yellow and blue), packed into a cardboard tube, but the tube was replaced by a much more fitting plastic barrel in 1968.

As you might expect, building a chain of 12 monkeys is tricky (anything involving monkeys usually is) but the simplicity of the concept, and the fact that it can just as easily be enjoyed in solitary play as competitively, means that kids just never tire of trying.

RUBIK'S CUBE

1980
Inventor: Erno Rubik
www.rubiks.com

There are lots of cool words in this book. 'Zectron', 'aliphatic' and 'hypotrochoids' spring to mind, but for sheer impressiveness, 'quintillion' will take some beating. The *Rubik's Cube*, invented by Hungarian professor of architecture Erno Rubik, has 43 quintillion possible combinations.

Clearly, with so many permutations, actually solving the *Rubik's Cube* is impossible, so we might as well move on... except that it isn't impossible. In fact, people have been known to solve it in less time than it takes Usain Bolt to cover 100 metres.

Endless articles and books have been written delving into the remarkable mathematical and mechanical properties of the deceptively simple cube, but all the user is really concerned with is finding a way to restore it to its original state, with a solid block of colour on each of its six sides. And if you use a step-by-step guide it doesn't count.

Although Rubik is famously reluctant to talk about his invention, in 2010 he gave a brief interview to mark the 30th anniversary of its release on a previously well-adjusted and angst-free world, and he managed to hit the nail on the head regarding the cube's addictive qualities.

"It mirrors life," said the professor (raising the alarming prospect of our lives being a chaotic jumble that defies all attempts to impose order unless we buy a book that tells us what to do). "From the beginning of our lives, we try to simplify the complexities of the world and nature so that we can understand them."

For most of us, beating Usain Bolt would be easier.

JACKS

www.houseofmarbles.com

Many toys and games allow children to create their own little worlds. The game of *Jacks* has created its own language. This ancient game (variations have been played with pieces of wood, bone or pebbles for thousands of years, and it's been known as '*Dibs*', 'China clay' and 'Sharp crackers') comes with a dictionary as impenetrable to the outsider as Cockney rhyming slang.

'Twosies', 'threesies', 'pigs in the pen' and 'flying Dutchman' all have special meanings in this game, which is actually far simpler than the language that surrounds it.

The classic *Jacks* game involves a bouncy rubber ball and a number of metal 'jacks' – six-pointed constructions that can be easily picked up in one hand. This is critical, because the game involves that, and little else.

After either throwing the ball in the air or bouncing it off a flat surface, players attempt to pick up the jacks one at a time before catching the ball in the same hand. As the game progresses, the player will attempt to pick up two, three or more jacks at a time.

Playable as a solitaire game, it also works perfectly as a competitive endeavour, with players competing to reach higher up the *Jacks* chart of achievement. It can also be played anywhere that a flat surface can be found and, with all the necessary equipment fitting easily into a pocket or a little bag, it's a supremely portable game, whatever you choose to call it.

JENGA

1983
Inventor: Leslie Scott
www.hasbro.com

Although launched at the London Toy Fair in 1983, *Jenga* had been 'in development' for over a decade prior to that, having started out as a family game created by Leslie Scott while living in Ghana in the 1970s.

On her return to the UK, Scott demonstrated the game to friends while studying at Oxford and decided to market the game under her own name. The game was a success and distribution deals were soon in place to turn it into a global phenomenon. An estimated 50 million *Jenga* sets have since been sold worldwide.

Using 54 identical wooden blocks, the game involves removing individual blocks from the starting point of an 18-storey tower (each storey is comprised of three blocks) and placing them on top, thus adding to the height of the tower while also increasing instability.

Scott, who was fluent in Swahili, christened her game *Jenga*, which is the Swahili word for 'build', although it's actually the toppling over bit that marks the end of the game.

Jenga requires nothing more than a modicum of manual dexterity, although if you have an engineering bent you could probably sketch out some effective strategies for ensuring you aren't the player who brings the tower crashing down.

The record for the highest tower constructed is claimed by Robert Grebler, who took over US and Canadian distribution in 1984 (and doubtless got lots of practice in while demonstrating it to potential stockists). Grebler is reported to have built a *Jenga* tower of 40 stories, so that's something to aim for.

MOUSE TRAP

1963
Inventors: Gordon Barlow and Burt Meyer
www.hasbro.com

Build a better mouse trap, they say, and the world will beat a path to your door, but Marvin Glass & Associates didn't enjoy instant success with this wacky game, designed around an insanely complicated rodent catcher.

The first company the game was offered to, Milton Bradley, turned it down, but Ideal saw its potential and the result was one of the first three-dimensional board games. It is as much toy as game because of the mouse trap itself. The rules of the original version called for the trap to be assembled as the game progressed, but many children bypassed this stage altogether and simply constructed the trap to watch it in action. (The current version has the trap assembled from the start.)

Inspired by the cartoonist Rube Goldberg, the secret of *Mouse Trap*'s success is that the trap actually works, and that's no mean feat when you consider that pieces had to be cheaply made to keep the game affordable and profitable. The careful design that went into each component is evident when you set the metal ball rolling along the 22 interconnecting pieces, setting in motion a train of events that eventually captures an unsuspecting mouse (though how it could be unsuspecting with all that racket going on is a mystery) under a basket.

The mouse trap inspired by Goldberg was also humane, and the captured mouse could soon be up and about again, ready to take its chances in another game.

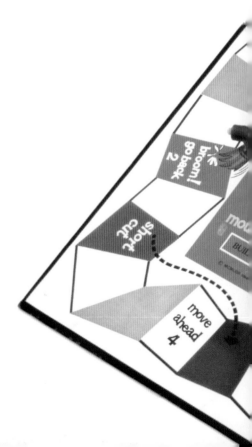

1963 *Mouse Trap*, by Ideal.

MARBLES

www.houseofmarbles.com

It is believed that the first marbles were made from clay in India during the era of the Harappan civilisation (three and a half to five thousand years ago), but the game of marbles has no doubt been played for much longer than that, using pebbles and balls of clay.

When we think of marbles today, however, we think of the small, colourful glass marbles that were originally available only to the wealthy. That changed around 1846, when a German glassblower (the impressively named Elias Johann Christoph Simon Carl Greiner), invented 'marble scissors', which made it easier (and cheaper) to craft these glass spheres. Marbles became much more widely available and mass-production techniques quickly followed.

The standard game involves arranging a group of marbles in a marked out area (usually a circle) and then using bigger 'shooter' or 'tolley' marbles to knock them out of the ring. This is the format used at the annual World Marbles Championships, which have been held at Tinsley Green in West Sussex since 1932, although countless other game variants have also been developed.

Aside from the game itself, many people love marbles simply for their aesthetic qualities (the Japanese dreamed up the addition of coloured glass in the centre) and more than one astronaut is credited with realising that, viewed from space, the Earth looks like nothing more than a beautiful big blue marble.

BATTLESHIP

1931
Inventor: Clifford Von Wickler
www.hasbro.com

*B*attleship started life as a simple pen-and-paper game over a hundred years ago (and can still be enjoyed in this format today). Created in the early 20th century, its first official incarnation was as 'Broadsides', from Milton Bradley, in 1931.

A lot of games are a bit hit or miss, but Battleship takes this to literal lengths. The game involves hunting down your opponent's fleet at the same time as they seek out yours, lobbing speculative shots around a marked-out grid and hoping to hit something other than the deep blue sea.

The game has since taken on more tangible form, with little plastic ships now trying to disappear within plastic seas, as white and red pegs mark out unsuccessful and (gulp) successful

shots. Tension builds like a black-and-white World War II film as salvoes land ever closer to your fleet, while your enemy remains elusive (and any aficionado will happily tell you that the aircraft carrier, not the battleship, is the most important piece on the board).

The subject of a brilliant advertising campaign in the 1970s, in which a pair of dinner-jacketed gentlemen find the game far more interesting than a boring old opera, many people are now unable to play without calling out 'You sank my battleship!' at the critical moment.

Upgrades to electronic and PC versions, as well as the adoption of various licenses (*Star Wars Battleships* being a good example), haven't really added much to a game that didn't need any help in the first place.

ROCK 'EM SOCK 'EM ROBOTS

1964
Inventors: Burt Meyer, Harry Disko and Judd Reed
www.mattel.com

'Ladies and gentlemen! This is your main event of the evening (or afternoon if it isn't a school day)! In the red corner, the Red Rocker! In the blue corner, the Blue Bomber! Let's get ready to rumble!'

In the future, robots may do the ironing and clean the house, but how much more fun would it be if they would climb into a boxing ring and start swinging at each other? *Rock 'em Sock 'em Robots* took this fascinating proposition and made it real, in plastic form. The Red Rocker and Blue Bomber (controlled by two human 'managers') would lay into each other with wild abandon until one of them had his block knocked off.

A toy that was tailor-made for TV commercials, *Rock 'em Sock 'em Robots* actually played well too and was commendably faithful to the concepts of boxing. There was room for different boxing styles (float like a butterfly or unleash the haymakers) and even the most unskilled player had a puncher's chance, although if robot pugilists were ever invented it is unlikely they would have built-in glass jaws.

Marketed under the sublime name 'Raving Bonkers' in the UK, the original Marx toy was relaunched by Mattel in 2000 with smaller robots – no doubt following weeks in the gymnasium to make the new weight.

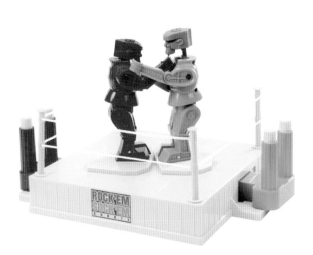

Original *Rock 'em Sock 'em Robots*, by Marx.

2001 *Rock 'em Sock 'em Robots*, by Mattel.

LABYRINTH

1946
www.brio.net

BRIO is a name usually associated with toy trains (and, indeed, appears again in our trains section, see page 176), but it was the marble game *Labyrinth* that put the company on the map in the 1950s.

When the three sons of Swedish basket merchant Ivar Bengtsson took over the company business in Osby in 1908, they registered it as 'Brothers Ivarsson Osby' – BRIO. A wooden horse had already been produced as the company's first toy, and this side of the business expanded steadily until, in 1946, *Labyrinth* was released, over ten years before BRIO's first wooden railway.

The labyrinth has a rich history in mythology, most famously in the story of Theseus and the Minotaur. Theseus's maze was anything but fun – there was a Minotaur in it, after all – but strip away the danger of being eaten alive and the entertainment value is clear, which is why mazes are popular tourist attractions around the world.

BRIO's maze is constructed from wood, with a marble waiting to be guided through the twists and turns. Two dials, one on each side, tilt the playing surface, allowing the skilful player to move the marble steadily

through the maze (the unskilful player will likely see their marble disappear down the first hole – not as frightening as running into a Minotaur, but just as effective at ending the game). Acknowledging that *Labyrinth* can be tricky, BRIO also offers a version with two simpler mazes for younger players to enjoy.

Widely copied, BRIO's *Labyrinth* remains a classic in the wooden toy world. More than three million copies of the original have been sold.

SUBBUTEO

1947
Inventor: Peter Adolph
www.hasbro.com

There are established rules in place for launching a new toy. One of them states that you should have a product ready for sale before you advertise it, but that didn't stop Peter Adolph from placing an ad for his *Subbuteo* football game in *Boy's Own Paper* in 1946. The advert offered to send details of a game that wouldn't actually go on sale until the following year.

When the game was available it arrived as an 'assembly outfit' — the purchaser was expected to cut out the cardboard football players and attach them to the plastic bases (weighted buttons) and then mark out a pitch on an army blanket using the thoughtfully provided piece of chalk.

It doesn't sound like an auspicious start, but *Subbuteo* had two big elements in its favour. First of all, it tapped into the limitless appeal of football. Secondly, the game worked remarkably well, employing a 'flick to kick' method that resulted in engrossing games.

Evolution involved new player designs (including characterless creations from the 1970s known to collectors as 'zombies'), the provision of pitches and a whole slew of accessories, including policemen, scoreboards and even streakers.

By far the most popular element, of course, is the ability to buy a set of players wearing the strip of your favourite team. International and club sets appeal to collectors as well as fans, though we're not quite sure who the streaker figures are meant to appeal to…

Vintage *Subbuteo* equipment.

1970s *Subbuteo* heavyweight players.

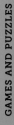

JIGSAW PUZZLES

1767
Inventor: John Spilsbury
www.ravensburger.com

From their beginnings as an educational aid, to the vast proliferation of designs and shapes we have today, jigsaw puzzles have been entertaining us since 1767. English mapmaker and engraver John Spilsbury is generally credited with creating the first jigsaw puzzle when he stuck one of his world maps onto a piece of wood and cut around the borders of the countries with a marquetry saw. The result was an extremely useful teaching aid to help children get a grip on global geography, although these first creations were known as 'dissections' rather than jigsaws.

The rather clinically named dissections remained educational tools until around 1820 and only took on the name 'jigsaw puzzles' around 1880 — even then it was a fretsaw, not a jigsaw, that was used to cut out the pieces, a lesson in the basic fact that credit doesn't always go where it should when it comes to inventions.

Most people know that the best way to complete a puzzle is to first put the straight-edged pieces together and then use the picture on the box as a guide. In a sort of jigsaw puzzle arms race, manufacturers have managed to keep one step ahead of the public with various strategies and today you can buy spherical puzzles with no edge pieces at all, puzzles without a guiding picture, fiendish double-sided puzzles and even a massive 32,000-piece puzzle that nobody has the room to put together.

Fittingly, you can still buy 'dissected' world maps, just like the one John Spilsbury created more than 250 years ago.

OPERATION

1965
Inventor: John Spinello
www.hasbro.com

'Death Valley' doesn't sound like the name of a legendary toy, but that's how *Operation* started out after student John Spinello invented the basic concept as an industrial design project. Selling his idea to MGA for $500, the game was developed as a hunt for water in a desert landscape (sounds like great fun), and it was only when Milton Bradley took over the rights that the focus was switched to the operating theatre.

Instead of probing water holes in the desert, players now probed an unfortunate patient known as 'Cavity Sam', trying to sort out an extensive list of afflictions including water on the knee, writer's cramp and broken heart. Nobody paid any attention to what was clearly Sam's most important ailment – a horribly swollen nose that glowed red and buzzed whenever the 'surgeon' made a mistake.

Whether or not *Operation* has inspired any children to become surgeons is debateable, but it may well have launched the career of a few interrogation specialists, because the game seems to bring out a devilish side in children — it is most enjoyable when the surgery goes wrong.

Recent versions have taken advantage of this. The Homer Simpson game, for example, positively encourages little sawbones to torment their helpless patient as Homer unleashes a repertoire of blood-curdling screams and shouts, including the deeply disconcerting 'I'm awake! I'm awake!'.

With SpongeBob Square Pants, Spider-Man, Iron Man, the Hulk, the Daleks and Buzz Lightyear all taking their place on the operating table, this is one surgeon's list that will take a while to get through.

Original 1965 *Operation*, US version.

MASTERMIND

1971
Inventor: Mordecai Meirowitz
www.pressmantoy.com

*M*astermind (originally known as Master Mind) is a code-breaking game that's nothing to do with the UK TV show (although the box image does look a little like a contestant awaiting his questioning by Magnus Magnusson).

Players take it in turns to set a secret code, made up of coloured pegs and hidden behind a small screen. The code breaker must then discover the hidden code, making attempts and receiving feedback in the form of black and white mini pegs. The game progresses until the code is cracked, with the idea being to take as few turns as possible.

There were six peg colours and four holes in each row in the original, but later versions made things more difficult by adding more holes and/or colours. Number and word versions of the game have been tried but are somehow less satisfying (a number version was also issued in electronic form).

The basics of Mordecai Meirowitz's invention (he was an Israeli postmaster) are so easy to grasp that *Mastermind* is often cited as a game that transcends the language barrier, but its simplicity was lost on the first toy companies Meirowitz approached with his idea.

Following numerous rejections, he showed the game to a small Leicester-based company, Invicta Plastics, at the 1971 Nuremburg Toy Fair. Following some developmental tweaks, the game went on to be named Game of the Year in 1973 and has sold over 50 million copies worldwide in its various guises.

1973 *Master Mind*, by Vic-Toy (Invicta).

TIDDLYWINKS

1888
Inventor: Joseph Assheton Fincher
www.tiddlywinks.org

Although tiddlywinks had been played before, Joseph Assheton Fincher applied for a patent on the game in 1888 (it was granted in 1889), applying later for a trademark on the name 'Tiddledy Winks', which was also approved. Whatever the game was known as, it enjoyed one of the most spectacular periods of popularity witnessed in the annals of toy history.

Fincher's patent, in fact, was merely the starting pistol for a flurry of applications over the following years, for endless versions of the game, as tiddlywinks fever took hold. Tennis, baseball, golf, football (both American and English versions) and basketball were among the sports given the tiddlywinks treatment. Military applications followed in the 20th century, with *Battle Winks* and *Tiddledy-Winks at Sea*, while the game had descended into toilet humour (literally) by 1996 with Gibsons Games' *Widdly Winks*.

It would be easy to get the idea that tiddlywinks is not a game to be taken seriously, but it can lay claim to being the most versatile entry in this book – like insects in the Amazon, you don't have to look too hard to find a new variety.

Through all the formats and variations, one element has remained constant – the propelling of the smaller counters by means of pressing down on them with a larger one. Whether you're aiming for a pot, a pile of other tiddlywinks or the baseline of centre court, there is skill involved in this, as well as a dose of luck, making the game both easy to play and difficult to master – the fundamental element of so many timeless games.

3 Activity toys

BALLS
KITES
SLINKY
BUBBLE BLOWER
RADIO FLYER WAGON
NERF
SKIPPING ROPE
STYLOPHONE
HULA HOOP
TWO TUNE TV
FRISBEE
POGO STICK
SUPER BALL
VIEW-MASTER
JACOB'S LADDER
SPACE HOPPER
ROCKING HORSE
YO-YO

BALLS

Throw it, kick it, catch it, hit it, roll it, bounce it – the ball has been with us for millennia and was probably 'invented' when an early caveman saw how a particularly spherical stone rolled rather pleasingly down a hill.

Arguably the most universally appealing toy, you can play with a ball on your own, as a group or as part of an organised team. You can get the family dog to join in (try getting it to play *Mastermind*) and even a cat might waft a paw at one as it rolls by.

The ball, with its spherical form, is the nearest thing to perfection in the world of toys, echoing the shape of celestial bodies. Billiard balls, soccer balls, golf balls, cricket balls, tennis balls and more have all been adapted for their role in a particular sport – designed to fly truer, further, higher – yet share the same basic, beautiful shape. Every four years, a ball becomes a talking point for billions as the new World Cup football is unveiled, invariably to criticism that it is now too light, too unpredictable in the air... too *round*.

Balls are not all round, of course. Elongated along one axis, prolate spheroids are used in rugby, American football and Australian Rules football and are carried purposefully to the park by youngsters aiming to emulate their heroes.

Balls are a genuine generation-bridger, and the timeless tradition of a parent playing catch with his child is so enduring an entire film was once made about it. As Ray Kinsella said, voice cracking with emotion, at the end of *Fields of Dreams*, "Hey, Dad? You wanna have a catch?"

KITES

www.brookite.com

The exact origin of kites is a matter of debate (some say they originated in China around 2,800 BC, others that Indonesians were using leaf-based kites much earlier), but whichever is the case, the kite is possibly the most useful toy ever invented.

From Benjamin Franklin's proposed experiment to prove that lightning is a form of electricity, to observation kites used by the military, the kite has countless purposes. It has measured wind speed, powered vehicles, inspired more than a few magnificent men to build flying machines and even hoisted people up into the air for a variety of purposes.

In the world of play, the applications are hardly less varied. There are stunt kites, enormous animal-shaped kites, racing kites, fighting kites and miniature kites. They fly alone, in synchronised pairs, or in huge colonies. At the bottom end of the

technology scale, kids can even make their own kites quite easily using nothing more than paper, string and lightweight wooden sticks.

Most people find them easy to fly, which is a big part of their charm – even toddlers can enjoy holding a piece of string if there's a kite soaring at the other end. Kites are so easy to use, in

fact, that when Charles M. Schulz was looking for a symbol of Charlie Brown's intrinsic haplessness, he chose his inability to fly a simple paper kite.

SLINKY

1945
Inventor: Richard James
www.poof-slinky.com

Few toys can boast a CV as colourful as that of the *Slinky*. It was the subject of one of the longest-running advertising jingles in history ('What walks down stairs, alone or in pairs, and makes a slinkity sound?'), has been taken into orbit aboard the Space Shuttle, has had its own postage stamp and is the official state toy of Pennsylvania.

That's not bad for a toy that was 'invented' by accident, when naval engineer Richard James was experimenting with springs and watched with interest when one of his test subjects fell to the floor in a series of steps. Two years later, in 1945, his new toy was demonstrated at Gimbels Department Store in Philadelphia. Named by James' wife, Betty, the first batch of 400 *Slinkys* sold out in 90 minutes. Sales have since topped the 300 million mark, although most of the early profits were wiped out when inventor James left his wife, family and company to join a religious cult in Bolivia, having previously sent them thousands of dollars.

The *Slinky* is most famed for its ability to walk down stairs, powered by nothing more than gravity and its own momentum. It's not a concept that is easily explained, but when seen in action the appeal is instant (a demonstration on a sloping surface at Gimbels was the key to that first sell-out).

Spin-offs have included the *Slinky Dog*, which launched in 1952 and features in the *Toy Story* movie franchise, the *Slinky Train* and *Crazy Eyes* glasses. There are, perhaps inevitably, plastic versions as well, but they really are missing the point – they don't deliver that 'slinkity' sound.

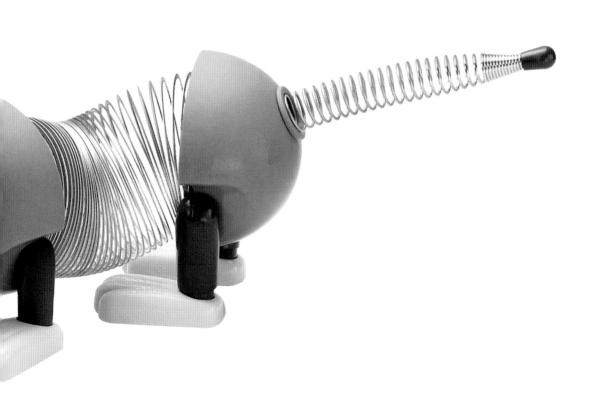

BUBBLE BLOWER

www.elc.co.uk

It's impossible to know who first decided that bubbles could be blown for fun (probably the first person to ever see one), but a 1733 painting by Jean-Siméon Chardin shows a boy blowing a bubble through a straw. In the 18th century, bubbles were thought to be representative of the fragility of life, but such morbid thoughts have no place here – bubble blowers have proved one of the most enduring of all toys because of the simple pleasure they bring.

Whether you enjoy chasing bubbles to pop them, or simply marvelling at the swirl of colours on their surface, bubbles have a special appeal and the range of blowers created over the centuries is truly astounding.

Bubble blowers exist in an almost endless variety of

forms. There are the basic pipes and blowers (where you have to provide the puff yourself), wand types (where a casual wave of the hand can produce dozens of bubbles) and even mechanised versions (which remove the hands-on fun but make up for this by generating stunning amounts of bubbles).

Wham-O's *Zillion Bubble Blower* is perhaps the most famous. Created in 1968, it looked a bit like a table tennis bat with holes in. When loaded up with bubble mixture this wouldn't exactly make a zillion bubbles, but it would make enough for it to seem churlish to complain.

Zillion Bubbles advert.

The brilliance of the bubble blower, however, rests in the fact that you don't need to invest in the latest gadgetry to enjoy bubble-fuelled antics. Twist a piece of wire, mix some water with washing-up liquid, and you're off.

Monster Bubbles®
and Zillion Bubbles®

New, delightful packaging for a classic favorite.

Here's three great toys in one . . . a monster wand for monster bubbles, a zillion paddle for zillions of bubbles and an in-betweener wand for in-betweener bubbles.

MAKES THREE KIDS HAPPY!

Also includes a bubble dish and bottle of bubble fluid.
Makes for hours of enjoyment for one to three youngsters.

Now charmingly packaged in a gift-quality shadow box.

NEW PACKAGE GRAPHICS

Stock No. 7482
Individual Pack: 1 each
Master Shipping Carton: 24

®Monster Bubbles and Zillion Bubbles are registered trademarks of Wham-O Mfg. Co.
U.S. Patent No. 3,295,248
©1981 Wham-O Mfg. Co., San Gabriel, Calif. 91778.

RADIO FLYER WAGON

1923
Inventor: Antonio Pasin
www.radioflyer.com

Italian-born Antonio Pasin earned the nickname 'Little Ford' for his innovation and use of mass-production techniques as founder of the Liberty Coaster Manufacturing Company in Chicago. Originally working with wood, the company switched to stamped steel and became Radio Steel & Manufacturing. The company's first steel wagon was named the *Radio Flyer*, reflecting Pasin's fascination with flight and the invention of the radio by fellow Italian Guglielmo Marconi.

An eye-catching exhibit at the 1933 World's Fair, in Chicago, helped to put the company firmly on the map, and the following decades saw the *Radio Flyer* wagon cement its place as an icon of American childhood.

The key to the *Radio Flyer*'s success was that it was not built as a toy, but as a serious piece of equipment that would last for years. In the forties, the Congo Thousand Mile Bearing was incorporated into the design, promising to deliver a thousand miles of smooth running. That was enough for most kids.

Radio Flyer wagons are able to keep pace with the imaginations of the children who play with them – transporting their toys to a friend's house, riding down hills dreaming of being a pilot, or simply being pulled along on the wagon by an obliging brother or sister.

Although many colour schemes have been produced (including a blue Mickey Mouse version and a yellow Evel Knievel offering), it is the little red wagon that has endured.

Liberty Coaster wagon and company founder Antonio Pasin.

NERF

1969
Inventor: Reyn Guyer
www.hasbro.com

Original *Nerf* Indoor Ball

Although the *Nerf* ball seems like an obvious toy – giving kids the freedom to play ball games inside without fear of breaking every valuable object in the house and possibly bringing the roof down – the story of its invention isn't quite that simple. As is so often the case, there was bit of luck involved, and one of those 'eureka' moments that has given us so many great inventions.

When working on the design for a caveman-themed game, including foam rocks, Reyn Guyer had a flash of inspiration. The 'rocks' could be safely hurled around indoors and that was the key point of the game. Realising that the entire caveman theme was redundant, Guyer stripped the idea to its core and invented the *Nerf* ball.

The soft foam balls were an instant success, but the idea has grown remarkably since that first stroke of genius. Having been stripped down,

the concept has since been built up again. A new foam construction material allowed the *Nerf* football to arrive in 1972. Able to be thrown and kicked just like a real football, it was actually too solid to be used indoors any more, but it meant that youngsters could emulate their NFL heroes in the back yard or park without needing to wrestle with heavy leather footballs.

The 'Nerfoop' basketball game is a natural extension of this, but the intervention of Lonnie Johnson (see also *Water Pistols*, page 136) took *Nerf* in a whole new direction, introducing dart-firing guns with soft-tipped *Nerf* darts.

The world's first indoor ball has come a long way.

SKIPPING OR JUMP ROPE

www.jumprope.com

Skipping is believed to have started as a play activity in China, Egypt or Australia, with vines as the first ropes. The simple pleasure derived from skipping or jumping rope has ensured that it has endured over centuries.

Aside from the fun involved, skipping also has considerable health benefits and is used as part of the training regimens of professional athletes. It is considered to be a safer form of exercise than jogging and more beneficial to the cardiovascular system – but this is beside the point when it comes to children, who can enjoy skipping rope alone or in groups, for simple play, or competitively.

Although the basic form of the skipping rope has understandably remained a constant, the number of ways it is enjoyed has expanded greatly, with a whole vocabulary of moves and games now associated with one of the simplest toys there is.

'Inverse toad', 'Criss-cross' and 'Awesome Annie' describe moves in an emerging sport that, on one level, is growing more serious all the time, while the familiar schoolyard game retains its more innocent nature, even when things are complicated by the addition of a second rope (Double Dutch).

Perhaps surprisingly, originally jumping rope was a male-dominated pastime as young girls were discouraged from over-exerting themselves. With childhood obesity a major issue in the western world, attitudes have done an about-face and the emphasis has shifted towards encouraging children to get off their backsides and do some exercise. The skipping rope, as it has been for centuries, is only too willing to oblige.

STYLOPHONE

1968
Inventor: Brian Jarvis
www.recreationplc.com

Any toy would be successful with the benefit of a Rolf Harris advertising campaign, but the *Stylophone* had more than that going for it. Invented by Brian Jarvis, who was co-founder of a dubbing and recording studio (dub/rec, 'Dubreq'), the *Stylophone* offered a distinctive sound and was incredibly easy to master.

Simply by moving the attached stylus up and down the metal keyboard you could produce a highly distinctive electronic noise, and with numbered 'keys' it was literally child's play to learn a tune.

Coming out at the tail end of the swinging sixties, this high-tech (for the day) gadget caught the eye of influential musicians including David Bowie and became something of a cult object (it even appeared in an episode of *Doctor Who*). Although production stopped in 1975, the *Stylophone* continued to be used by various musicians over the following decades and was finally resurrected

in 2007, with Brian Jarvis' son, Ben, at the helm of a re-launched Dubreq.

The *Stylophone* has the dubious honour of being known as the 'most annoying musical instrument of all time', but that seems unnecessarily mean-spirited for a product that has always been as much a toy as an actual musical instrument.

The new version does appear to take this unwelcome accolade into account, however. Unlike the original, today's *Stylophone* has a volume control.

1970 *Stylophone* Latin American Album, by Dubreq.

HULA HOOP

1958
Inventors: Arthur 'Spud' Melin and Richard Knerr
www.wham-o.com

The subject of one of the biggest toy crazes of all time, the *Hula Hoop* was actually nothing new when Arthur 'Spud' Melin and Richard Knerr created the first plastic hoop in 1958. Earlier hooping crazes had gripped England in the 19th century (although those hoops were made of wood and rolled along the ground) and hoops appear in Greek and Roman art.

The 1958 incarnation, however, really struck a nerve. Wham-O (the company behind the *Frisbee*, see page 94) sold more than 100 million in the first year of production, a truly staggering figure. The craze ignited partly because of the affordability of the *Hula Hoop* (it was priced at $1.98) and partly because you could just do so many things with it.

1960s Hula Hoop competition.

In fact, over the next few years it seemed as if all Americans wanted to do was invent new ways to play with these simple plastic hoops. Records were quickly set for endurance hooping, for the number of hoops spun simultaneously, for the largest hoop used. The Soviets condemned the *Hula Hoop* as a symbol of American decadence, and they were probably right.

Sadly, a craze can only burn for so long, and the *Hula Hoop* fad began to fade after just a couple of years, allowing America to concentrate on more important things, like putting a man on the moon. But the *Hula Hoop* never really went away and although the world may never again be gripped by such a fever, predictions of a new craze appear regularly in the media.

1967 Hula Hoop advert.

TWO TUNE TV

1966
www.fisher-price.com

In today's multi-channel TV world it's hard to imagine that a set showing the same two (exceedingly brief) programmes on a never-ending loop would be able to capture a youngster's attention. The Fisher-Price *Two Tune TV* did just that and, for that matter, is still doing it, thanks to its timeless charm.

This would present a real challenge to a TV schedule copywriter. Today's viewing starts with 'Row, Row, Row Your Boat', followed by 'London Bridge is Falling Down'. There's more fun on the river in 'Row, Row, Row, Your Boat', but later tension rises as London Bridge appears to be in imminent danger of collapse. Staying with the river theme, we then have another chance to see the classic 'Row, Row, Row, Your Boat', before my fair lady is informed of a disaster on the Thames...

Despite the predictability, children stare, transfixed, at this little plastic TV as the beautiful pictures scroll by and the music plays. Part of the appeal is the fact that the kids are, to some extent, in control. They must wind the TV up for the programmes to broadcast, and there's fun to be had in trying to guess at exactly what point the thing will stop.

Proof, if ever it were needed, that kids have too much TV to choose from these days.

1966 *Two Tune TV*, by Fisher-Price.

FRISBEE

1948
Inventor: Walter Morrison and Warren Franscioni
www.wham-o.com

In 1947, rumours of a UFO crashing near Roswell in the United States sparked a nationwide obsession with visitors from outer space. Hoping to cash in on this, Walter Morrison and Warren Franscioni rebranded their own plastic disk invention in 1948, calling it the 'Flying Saucer'. We know it better as the *Frisbee*, which is what their creation was renamed in 1958.

This brought the toy (almost) back to its alleged roots – the Frisbie Baking Company pie plates hurled by American university students towards the end of the 19th century. The Wham-O company proved that those students were on to something. *Frisbees* were great fun and, with that curved outer edge (the 'Morrison slope') they were also remarkably aerodynamic.

Frisbee-flinging sports soon started to appear, most notably 'Ultimate', which now boasts millions of players around the world. Ultimate epitomises the counter-culture ethos of the *Frisbee*, with most games played without the need for officials.

The *Frisbee*'s main strength, however, is the fact that it can be enjoyed by one, two or more people, of almost any age, in almost any environment, and a vast proliferation of colours and styles ensures there is a *Frisbee* to suit everyone's taste.

Often used as a generic term to apply to all flying disc toys, the *Frisbee* has attained an almost universal recognition status, ensuring that whatever the future holds for it, it will never be an unidentified flying object.

1965 *Frisbee* advert.

POGO STICK

1919
Inventor: George B. Hansburg
www.pogostick.org.uk

The origins of the pogo stick are uncertain, with similar contraptions appearing ever since the end of the 19th century, but it was in 1919 that George B. Hansburg applied for a patent for his 'Pogo Stick'.

Hansburg delighted in telling the story of a Burmese girl whose father invented a jumping stick to enable her to safely travel to church. The girl's name was, so Hansburg's tall tale went, 'Pogo', but however the device got its name, it has proved to be a classic.

The first batch of pogo sticks, made of wood, rotted on their way to the US from Germany. Thankfully, this potential disaster merely prompted Hansburg to develop a more robust pogo stick, and his customer, Gimbels Department Store (who also displayed the first *Slinky* in 1945), was happy to play its part as midwife to another classic toy and didn't cancel the order.

Hansburg never stopped tinkering with his design. A new patent application in 1955 promised to create a pogo stick that was 'not likely to become deranged even with long use'. The same could not be said for anyone who chose to propel themselves around on one of these highly sprung wonders.

Still the subject of development, the latest pogo sticks promise to launch you up to six feet into the air, although a gasoline-powered version in the 1960s (the *Hop Rod*) proved every bit as dangerous as it sounds and was quickly discontinued.

SUPER BALL

1965
Inventor: Norman Stingley
www.wham-o.com

Super Ball testing and promotional images.

There was something very special going on at the Wham-O company around the middle of the 20th century. Creators of the *Hula Hoop* and *Frisbee*, two of the greatest toy crazes of all time, the company also brought us the insanely bouncy *Super Ball*.

This name was no vain boast. The *Super Ball*, like Super Man, is capable of leaping over buildings if hurled with sufficient force, and when simply dropped to a hard surface it bounces almost all the way back up.

These prodigious feats are perhaps not surprising for something made out of Zectron, a synthetic rubber with (here comes the science part) a high coefficient of restitution. Which means it is bouncy.

Zectron is also very hard, which means that bits of it are likely to break off as it careens around the universe, bouncing off anything that gets in its way. *Super Balls* bear their scars with pride, but they eventually impair the bounciness, which opened the way for imitations to steal much of the market. Though nowhere near as bouncy as the *Super Ball*, cheap imitations made of softer rubber lasted longer.

The original *Super Ball* was relaunched by Wham-O in 1998 and still appeals to the connoisseurs of the ball-bouncing fraternity. It also has one more achievement to boast of. When a name was being sought for the AFL-NFL championship game in the 1960s, AFL founder Lamar Hunt watched his children playing with their *Super Ball* and had a flash of inspiration. The Super Bowl was born.

AGES 5+

WHAM-O

THE INCREDIBLE

SuperBall®

BOUNCES UP TO 75FT (22.86m)

Made of Amazing ZECTRON!™

⚠ WARNING:
CHOKING HAZARD – Small balls.
Not for children under 3 years.

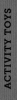

VIEW-MASTER

1938
Inventors: William Gruber and Harold Graves
www.fisher-price.com

The *View-Master*, a three-dimensional picture viewer, may never have become popular with children (and thus never have appeared in this book) if it hadn't been for its main competitor, the *Tru-Vue*.

Invented in 1938, the *View-Master* was targeted at a grown-up market, with its views of spectacular scenery, foreign cities and wildlife all presented in a highly effective 3D format. It was not of much interest to kids, who might enjoy the 3D effect for a while but would soon tire of the subject matter, and it wasn't until 1951, when *View-Master* took over *Tru-Vue*, that it made its first blip on children's radars.

The *Tru-Vue* acquisition added a sprinkling of magic in the form of its licensing agreement with Disney. The *View-Master* could now be used to look at Mickey Mouse, Donald Duck and Goofy rather than shots of Yellowstone National Park. The kids were suddenly interested.

The format retained an adult fan base as well (and there was even a *View-Master* personal stereo camera that allowed you to make your own 3D film discs), but gradually the *View-Master* became a toy, featuring reels of popular TV shows, movies and cartoon characters.

The *View-Master* has seen its place at the cutting edge of home entertainment technology undermined, yet it has somehow retained its place in the market due to the sheer novelty factor of those 3D views. Whether this appeal can stand up to the advent of 3D television in the home remains to be seen.

1959 Bugs Bunny *View-Master* reels, by Gaf.

JACOB'S LADDER

www.woodentoysuk.com

A stairway to heaven is a fairly impressive thing for a toy to be named after, especially one as simple as this classic wooden contraption.

In Genesis 28:12, the story is told of how Jacob fell asleep and dreamed of a ladder leading up to heaven, on which angels were ascending and descending. Interpretations of the passage vary (he may simply have been having a premonition about escalators in a shopping centre), but everyone is in agreement that the simple ribbon-and-block construction of the toy version allows for the blocks to move against each other in a baffling fashion, looking for all the world as if they are moving endlessly downwards, a bit like the ladder in Jacob's dream.

The optical illusion is made possible by the use of double-acting ribbon hinges and never fails to impress when first seen.

The origins of the toy are unclear, although the story that one was found in the tomb of King Tutankhamen is unsupported by evidence. It definitely dates back to the 19th Century at least, as it features in an 1889 edition of *Scientific American*.

'Jacob's Ladder' is also a term used to describe those arcing bolts of electricity between two metal rods that you see on old Frankenstein movies. These are most definitely not to be considered as toys.

SPACE HOPPER

1968
Inventor: Aquilino Cosani
www.wowstuff.co.uk

The *Space Hopper* is a triumph of expectation over experience. Since the 1960s children have stared in awe at these oversized orange balloons and imagined that they would be able to bounce to great heights (perhaps leaping tall buildings with a single bound) or career along at breakneck speed. The reality is that the *Space Hopper* makes it difficult to move anywhere at any sort of speed, and if you have a particular direction in mind things are trickier still.

The fact that none of this matters, and the fact that children will still clamber on board for another adventure at every opportunity, is down to the simple fact that the *Space Hopper* is an enormous amount of fun.

It is precisely the fact that you can't move quickly on them that makes *Space Hopper* races so enjoyable – the competitors desperately trying to stay upright and moving in the right direction is enough to reduce everyone, participants and spectators alike, to helpless laughter.

No official patent exists for the *Space Hopper*, but Italian Aquilino Cosani registered a patent in Italy in 1968 for his *Pon Pon*, an inflated rubber exercise ball with a rigid handle. The *Space Hopper* can be seen as a descendent of the *Pon Pon* and has been sold under many names, including the *Kangaroo Ball* (that face on the front is, apparently, meant to be a kangaroo), the *Hoppity Hop* and the *Hop Ball*.

Space Hoppers are now produced in a range of colours and sizes, and you can even double the fun on a tandem *Space Hopper*, which is nothing less than a stroke of genius.

ROCKING HORSE

18th century
www.rockinghorse.co.uk

The traditional rocking horse can trace its bloodline back through the hobby horse, rocking cradles and even training aids for medieval knights, but it wasn't until the 18th century that it started to establish itself as a children's toy.

While picking its way along the familiar path from expensive plaything for society's elite to mass-produced children's toy, the rocking horse attracted a very important admirer in the formidable shape of Queen Victoria, whose publicised preference for a dappled grey horse firmly established it as the most popular of all rocking horse variants.

Early versions sat on long wooden bows, which were equally effective at providing the rocking motion and trapping young toes, but in 1877 Phillip Marqua, of Cincinnati, Ohio, patented a safety stand, which caught on quickly and is now the standard mounting for a rocking horse.

The rocking horse is today available in a vast range of styles, including simple, plastic-moulded forms for toddlers. The horse is often replaced with a dog, a duck or even a dragon and these basic versions have resorted to the original bow rockers for ease of production and affordability.

The thoroughbred rocking horse still exists, but is once more an item for the richer elements of society, with beautiful, handcrafted horses often costing thousands of pounds. It's worth noting that you could buy a real horse for that, but wooden ones are much easier to clean up after.

Vintage Ayres rocking horse.

Charles I rocking horse.

YO-YO

www.wickedvision.co.uk

A Greek vase from around 440 BC apparently shows a boy playing with a yo-yo (did the ancient Greeks do nothing but play with toys?), although as the vase was crafted more than two millennia before the invention of three-dimensional moving pictures, it could simply be a ball on the end of a piece of string. Nobody doubts, however, that the yo-yo is a very old toy indeed, almost certainly pre-dating the Greek vase.

While some toys have remained essentially unchanged over decades or even centuries, the yo-yo is a toy that we just can't stop tinkering with. From the basic design (imperial, modified and butterfly are the most common, but many others exist) to the materials used (wood, plastic, aluminium, titanium), the yo-yo has steadily evolved. Since the invention of the 'take-apart' design, in 1978, users have been given free rein on how to set up their yo-yos.

Much of this will have passed unnoticed by children, who generally never progress far beyond an attempt to master the simple up-and-down motion with a basic yo-yo, but when players get more serious a new world opens up – a world of sleeping, looping, freehand and off-string (surely that must mean something's gone terribly wrong?) techniques.

Yo-yo popularity has charted an up-and-down path that reminds me of something I can't quite put my finger on. The first craze sparked up in 1929, when the Yo-yo Manufacturing Company of California cranked out 300,000 yo-yos each day. Following a steady decline after the Second World War, the yo-yo bounced back in the 1960s after a carefully orchestrated TV advertising campaign by the Duncan Toys Company, and, following another quiet spell, the yo-yo is once more a hot commodity today.

4 Role-play toys

DOLLS
Raggedy Ann

1918
Inventor: Johnny Gruelle
www.raggedy-ann.com

The doll is the archetypal girl's toy. Able to simultaneously provide comfort and an outlet for a nurturing soul, a doll is often a girl's most cherished possession – a confidante, friend and constant companion.

One very special doll also provided comfort to a grieving father, cartoonist Johnny Gruelle, following the death of his daughter, Marcella, in 1915. It was Marcella who (according to legend) had found an old ragged doll in the attic of the family house several years earlier. Gruelle painted on a fresh face and the doll became Marcella's favourite toy.

Following the tragic death of his daughter, Gruelle kept the raggedy doll in his studio, finally bringing her to life as *Raggedy Ann* in a book dedicated to his daughter's memory.

A doll followed quickly, with a winning combination of vulnerability and wide-eyed friendliness.

As if anyone could have ever doubted that *Raggedy Ann* had a heart, the stories explained that she had one made of candy. Early versions of the doll included a sewn-in piece of heart-shaped cardboard (some claim actual candy hearts were used on some dolls, although none has ever been found), while later versions opted for a printed version in the style of Love Hearts sweets.

As *Raggedy Ann* closes in on her first century, with a brother (*Raggedy Andy*, who appeared in 1920) to keep her company, she retains a special place in the world of dolls.

DOLLS
Barbie

1959
Inventor: Ruth Handler
www.barbie.com

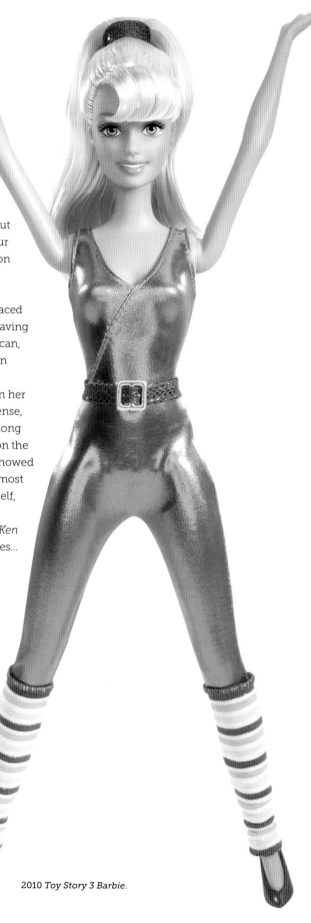

Ruth Handler spotted a gap in the market for a very different type of doll when she watched her daughter, Barbara, give adult roles to her paper dolls. Shop shelves in the 1950s were packed with baby dolls, but Handler realised that girls wanted more from their toys.

Inspired by the German Bild Lilli doll, Handler created a teenage fashion doll with a wardrobe of cutting edge ensembles designed by Mattel's Charlotte Johnson. *Barbie* (named after Handler's daughter) changed the way girls played with dolls and has kept pace with every fashion development for more than five decades.

Barbie has attracted controversy (not least because of her slim figure), but early criticism that she presented a limited range of career options for young girls has been well and truly dealt with — *Barbie* has enjoyed more than 125 careers, including astronaut (she made it into space four years before man walked on the Moon), surgeon and soccer star.

Barbie has also embraced a huge range of cultures, having appeared in African American, Hispanic, Chinese and even Eskimo versions.

Unsurprisingly, given her looks, fame and fashion sense, *Barbie* didn't have to wait long for a boyfriend to appear on the scene – Ken Carson first showed up in 1961, making him almost as enduring as *Barbie* herself, but after being an item for half a century, *Barbie* and *Ken* continue to live separate lives...

2011 *Barbie* and *Ken*.

2010 *Toy Story 3 Barbie*.

1980 Hispanic *Barbie* and 1965 Astronaut *Barbie*.

1959 Teenage Fashion Model
Barbie and 1960s *Barbie* and *Ken*.

DOLLS
Tiny Tears

1965
www.johnadams.co.uk

*T*iny Tears was exactly the sort of doll *Barbie* was created to contrast with. An American version launched in 1950, with two small holes on each side of her nose through which she could shed, yes, tiny tears, but it is the British *Tiny Tears*, which first appeared in 1965, that wins a place among our 100 classic toys. Palitoy's *Tiny Tears* could not only cry, she could wet herself as well – and nothing demonstrates more clearly the difference between boys and girls than the disparate reactions you'll get from each at such a feature.

Tiny Tears, the embodiment of helplessness (albeit a cheerful, smiley form of helplessness), tugged at little girls' heartstrings like nothing else. The more realistic a baby doll is, it seems, the better.

The story of *Tiny Tears* is bedevilled by one of the most torturous ownership histories in the toy world. General Mills, Playmates Toys, Kenner Parker and even Tonka have all been involved at different times, with John Adams & Toy Brokers currently marketing the latest *Tiny Tears*.

She's over 40 years old now and, like *Raggedy Ann*, she has a brother, *Timmy Tears*. Far from growing up, *Tiny Tears* has actually become even smaller, with *Teeny Tiny Tears* and even *Teeny Weeny Tiny Tears* appearing. It's difficult to see where she can go next.

DOLLS
Cabbage Patch Kids

1983
Inventor: Xavier Roberts
www.cabbagepatchkids.com

It's fitting that the final entry in the pantheon of classic dolls is the subject of one of the great urban legends regarding a toy (the story was that the *Cabbage Patch Kids* were created to prepare the public for the likelihood of birth defects following a nuclear war), because the real story is just one tall tale after another.

Inventor Xavier Roberts started working in 'soft sculpture' in the 1970s, using hand-stitched fabric to produce a variety of expressions on the face of a soft doll. With hand-painted details and real clothes, each of the 'Little People' he created was a labour of love – and highly desirable to doll enthusiasts and collectors.

Roberts' skills did not stop at the creation of his new dolls. He was also a gifted salesman and gradually concocted a rich story to promote them. The 'Little People' were not for sale, but you could adopt them (he produced adoption certificates to reinforce this). They were not made, but born in a hospital (Roberts and his staff took to wearing white coats during public appearances).

They didn't become *Cabbage Patch Kids* until 1983, when Coleco stepped in to offer mass-production techniques, making it possible to move three million units in the first year of sales of the rebranded dolls. A craze was now in full swing. In a Pennsylvania toy store in November 1983, a woman broke her leg when 1,000 Christmas-crazed customers stormed the shop in search of a few precious *Cabbage Patch Kids*. The store owner had to arm himself with a baseball bat.

Following several changes of production partners, the *Cabbage Patch Kids* are still being born today, and Xavier Roberts is still making hand-crafted versions. Urban myths are no longer needed – the truth is far more incredible.

FORTS AND CASTLES

www.letoyvan.com

Toy forts and castles have been around for centuries, but the earliest examples were unique, hand-made items, and it wasn't until the 19th century that they started to be manufactured commercially. This would have caused much excitement among the young boys of the day and was no doubt a relief to the growing legions of toy soldiers, who finally had somewhere to call home.

Production of play fortresses gathered momentum in the early years of the 20th century, with German company Moritz Gottschalk setting the early pace, and things really started to get interesting after World War 1, with Lines Brothers and Elastolin entering the market.

There has always been a dividing line between what might be termed authentic replicas and those made purely for play value. Airfix produced a selection of realistic, buildable dioramas for its 1:32 scale soldiers, including the famous *Desert Outpost*, and still offers sets for its smaller 1:72 range.

Companies like Playmobil and Le Toy Van, in contrast, are in it simply for the fun, with plastic and wooden castles and forts continuing to delight youngsters around the world.

Forts have always lived something of a double life. Whether made of wood, metal or plastic, they have served as both props for display and the focal point of fierce battles. They also make an excellent storage solution for a collection of toy soldiers – a fitting parallel to the existence of actual castles and forts, when you think about it.

BREYER

1950
www.breyerhorses.com

The first Breyer horse stood on top of a clock. The order for 2,000 ornamental horses had been welcomed by Breyer following the loss of its licence to produce custom-moulded plastic products for the U.S. government in 1950, and the reaction to the horse was enough to ensure that Breyer would follow a different path from that moment on.

With enthusiasts and hobbyists praising the horse for its accuracy, Breyer launched its first standalone model, totally independent of any timekeeping device. The *Western Horse* was to be the first in an illustrious line of equine models, including legendary names like Seabiscuit, Roy Rogers' Trigger, Secretariat, War Admiral and Locarno.

Although Breyer also produces accessories including barns, stables and horseboxes, the horses remain firmly centre stage. Breyer horses start life as sculptures by leading artists in the field, before being turned into copper and steel moulds, from which the cellulose acetate plastic models are created, one at a time, before being hand painted. No fewer than 20 people work on each model to ensure its accuracy is unrivalled.

Although girls are the obvious candidates for a love affair with Breyer, the company reports that boys are the most rapidly growing sector of their fan base and this is a fan base that embraces all aspects of the brand – the annual Breyerfest collector and equestrian festival, held in Lexington, Kentucky, attracts over 5,000 visitors.

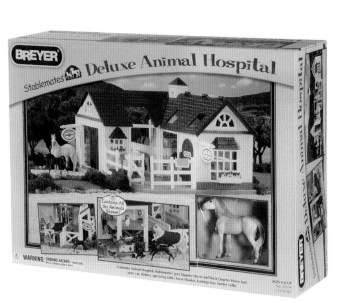

PLAYMOBIL

1974
Inventor: Hans Beck
www.playmobil.com

In 1974, Horst Brandstätter brought a small plastic figure to the Berlin Toy Fair. Known to its inventors as a 'Klicky', the figure stood just 2.9 inches high as a consequence of the 1970s oil crisis, which had pushed the price of plastic up by 600%. Wearing a smile and a wardrobe of three costumes — Indian, road worker and knight — the diminutive figure could have been forgiven for being a little shy, but that smile encapsulated everything that would make this one of the best-selling toys of all time. The Klicky, known to its millions of adoring fans as a *Playmobil* figure, was the first of 2.2 billion (and counting) 2.9-inch-high plastic figures to enthral children around the world.

The creation of designer Hans Beck, the strength of the *Playmobil* system was and remains the limitless play options offered by the little smiling characters. They have worn spacesuits, circus costumes, soldiers' uniforms and pirate hats. They have sailed in an Egyptian royal barge, called igloos, forts and castles home and enjoyed the company of elephants, dinosaurs and ghost whales, but the heart of the *Playmobil* system has always been the figures themselves and their never-ending willingness to embark on the next adventure.

Such was the near-perfection of the original idea that, despite the increasing extravagance of the themed worlds they inhabit, the only major change to the figures' basic design was the addition of moveable hands, in 1982. Early ideas to include a nose and even a frowning version were, thankfully, discarded — there is no room for frowns in the world of *Playmobil*.

1974 Road Worker *Playmobil* figure.

DOLLS HOUSE

16th Century
Inventor: Duke Albert V of Bavaria
www.dollshouse.com

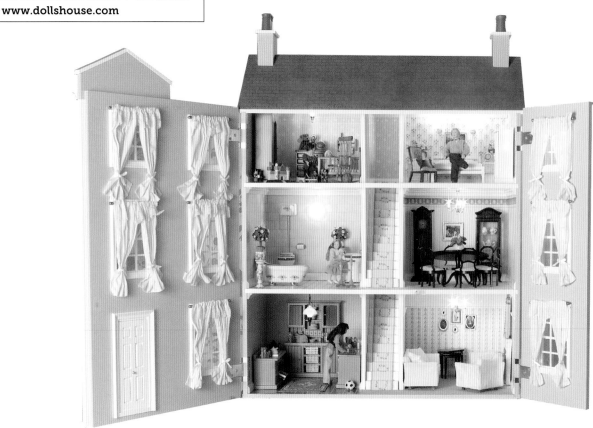

In the 16th Century, the Bavarian Duke Albert V commissioned a scale replica of his own house, which became known as his 'baby house' and sparked a new fashion throughout Europe.

As might be expected given this exalted beginning, dolls houses were not considered as toys, but as ways for the upper echelons of society to show off. It was only in the Victorian era, with the advent of mass production, that dolls houses arrived that were within the budget of the middle classes.

Built on a variety of scales, dolls houses were originally an educational aid as well as a plaything, teaching young girls about household management. They still appeal to adult collectors as well as children, with some of the more intricate replica furnishings being designed for display rather than play.

The 'traditional' dolls house is made of wood, although cheaper versions have been made out of sheet metal and plastic is sometimes used today. Children can also create their own versions using nothing more sophisticated than cardboard boxes, giving the term 'box room' a whole new meaning. Despite the name, the dolls themselves are strictly secondary to the fun of decorating and furnishing a miniature house.

Designs vary, but a staple layout features a hinged front that opens to reveal the detailed interior. Other types feature an open back and the roof may also lift off – loft conversions are very easy in the world of dolls houses.

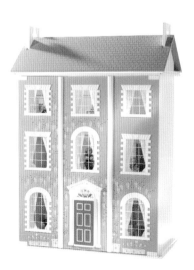

MR POTATO HEAD

1952
Inventor: George Lerner
www.hasbro.com

1950s *Mr Potato Head*.

In the beginning, there was a collection of plastic face and body parts, given away in cereal boxes. A toy company owned by Henry and Hillel Hassenfeld liked the idea and decided to market it under a new name. The plastic body parts became *Mr. Potato Head*. Hassenfeld Brothers became Hasbro.

It will surprise many to learn that *Mr. Potato Head* required the addition of an actual potato (or other fruit or vegetable) when he started out. More surprising still is the fact that this controversial use of food so soon after World War II persuaded many toy companies to pass on the idea, fearful of negative publicity.

The Hassenfeld Brothers pressed on regardless and were able to tap into a new medium to get their message across to millions of children. *Mr. Potato Head* was the first toy advertised on television – and the children who saw him wanted him.

Perhaps it is the inherently comical nature of a person with an oversized vegetable head that struck a chord with kids, or perhaps it was the whimsical nature of *Mr. Potato Head*'s rapidly growing family (*Mrs. Potato Head* joined him in 1953 and son *Spud* and daughter *Yam* soon followed).

Whatever the reason, kids had seldom had so much fun playing with their food and even though the current version substitutes a plastic potato for the real thing, the charm of *Mr. Potato Head* (now a major motion picture star, of course) endures.

G.I. JOE and ACTION MAN

1964
Inventor: Larry Reiner, Stan Weston and Don Levine
www.hasbro.com

1966
Inventor: Larry Reiner, Stan Weston and Don Levine
www.hasbro.com

At first glance, it may seem like *G.I. Joe* and *Action Man* are one and the same toy – they certainly started out that way, but the subsequent development of the toys in the US and UK, respectively, has taken them in vastly different directions, justifying (we think) including them as two toys.

In any case, they were so good they *deserve* two entries. Any toy that invents an entirely new category for the industry deserves extra marks, and it's medals all round for the creative geniuses who came up with *G.I. Joe*. Whoever you credit with the tag 'inventor' – Larry Reiner (who may have had the original spark of an idea), licensing agent Stan Weston (who may have had the idea himself and who certainly took it to Hasbro) or Don Levine (Hasbro's creative director, who developed the idea and made it a reality) – the end result is nothing short of toy industry folklore. We prefer to let them share the credit and get on with marvelling at their wondrous creation.

The idea of a doll for boys was considered laughable when a poseable soldier was first suggested, but despite this there was potential that couldn't be ignored. If the basic premise could be swallowed, it would open up tremendous new opportunities. Just as *Barbie* spawned an endless stream of accessories and outfits, so this soldier could be kitted out with different uniforms and military hardware.

An early idea of giving servicemen from different branches of the armed forces different names (including 'Rocky', the marine paratrooper) was thankfully shelved for the generic 'G.I. Joe', a catchall moniker for the common US serviceman. Spending millions to bring 'America's movable fighting man' (note the emphasis on 'movable') to market, Hasbro ran a very real risk of bankrupting itself if the toy failed. Four *G.I. Joes* – the *Action Sailor*, *Action Marine*, *Action Pilot* and *Action Soldier* – were mobilised for the 1964 Toy Fair in New York and were a huge success.

1964 *G.I. Joe.*

2010 Duke collectible action figure.

Two years later, *G.I. Joe* arrived in the UK, rebranded as *Action Man* and produced under licence by Palitoy. He was still the 'movable fighting man', although the term 'action figure' was now in use as well. A new sector in the toy market had opened up.

Britain's man of action initially came in three forms, with the marine being dropped. Although initially almost identical to his American cousin, *Action Man* soon began to follow his own path. Innovations like realistic hair, gripping hands and 'eagle eyes' would appear on *Action Man* first, before finding their way over the Pond to *G.I. Joe*.

But Joe had changed. Anti-military sentiment focussed on US involvement in the Vietnam War had seen sales fall dramatically just a few years after *G.I. Joe* first launched and, in 1969, he was rebranded as an all-round action hero, ditching the military theme altogether.

More pressure came from the smaller (and far less articulate) action figures from Kenner based on the *Star Wars* films (see page 146) and *G.I. Joe* slipped into a temporary retirement in 1977, to be reborn in the '80s on the back of a

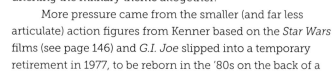

Marvel comic series. *G.I. Joe* was now the name of a band of elite fighters locked in a struggle with the evil Cobra organisation. The action figures associated with this line were in the same 3.75in. scale that Kenner had popularised.

Meanwhile, *Action Man* marched on in the UK, where the Vietnam War had far less of an impact. During a golden age in the '70s and early '80s *Action Man* was showered with uniforms, weapons and vehicles, including scout cars, helicopters and motorcycles. By 1984, however, he too had gone the way of *G.I. Joe*, relaunched as a scaled down action figure in a new and disappointing 'Action Force' range. In 1993 *Action Man* returned to full size, but in a non-military, 'action hero' theme echoing *G.I. Joe*'s much earlier conversion.

The spirit of *G.I. Joe* lives on in the stunning 12in. action figures from Sideshow Collectibles, while *Action Man* periodically dusts off his old uniforms in anniversary editions from Hasbro. These old soldiers, though they may sometimes fade away, will never die.

1960s and 1970s *Action Man* figures.

LITTLE PEOPLE

1950
www.fisher-price.com

As consumers, we always have the final say on whether a toy is successful or not. We do not, however, usually get to name the toy, yet Fisher-Price's *Little People* would still be the 'Play Family' were it not for the fact that we consumers simply called them... little people.

This whole toy line, in fact, had a lengthy gestation. Starting out with the Looky Fire Truck in 1950 (with three little firemen permanently attached), and evolving through the removable figures of 1959's *Safety School Bus* and 1960's *Nifty Station Wagon*, it wasn't until 1965 that the Play Family name was first used and it would take another 20 years before *Little People* was officially adopted.

The evolution of the figures

1959 Safety School Bus production line.

themselves has been equally eventful. The wooden peg people of the *School Bus* carried a lot of detail, most of

which was ditched for the much simpler family that came with the *Station Wagon*, while in 1991, for safety reasons, the now plastic figures saw their waistlines balloon to 'chunky' dimensions. In 1997 the figures became far more detailed and in 2000 they burst into song thanks to interactive electronic features.

Several sets have achieved legendary status, none more so than 1971's *Play Family School*, which included magnetic letters and numbers that could be arranged on the metal roof of the school building. A special edition of the school, launched to help celebrate the 50th anniversary of a line that officially started with the *Safety School Bus*, proved that these little people still have big appeal.

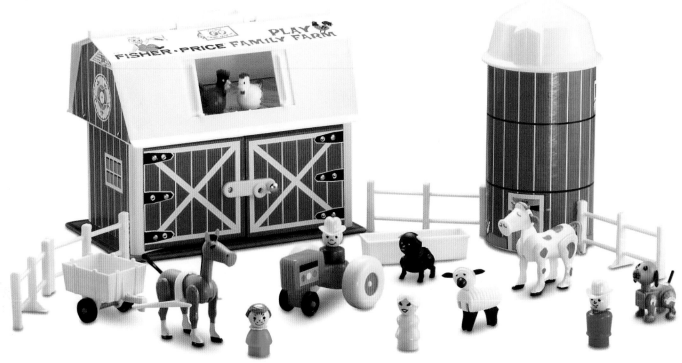
1961 Farm.

1971 School House.

SCHLEICH FIGURINES

1980
Inventor: Friedrich Schleich
www.schleich-s.com

Friedrich Schleich's company first started producing plastic figurines, based on the worlds of the Smurfs and Snoopy, in the 1950s, but it was 1980 that saw Schleich's most iconic range launch.

The production of a range of animals wasn't new; it was the extraordinary level of detail and beautiful, hand-painted colouring that made these new Schleich animals stand out. It is this detail that makes Schleich's animal figurines valuable both as role-play and educational toys. The detail even extends to the animals' feet – press a Schleich lion's paw into a piece of modelling dough and it will leave an authentic paw print. Compare that with the flat, featureless feet on cheaper plastic animals.

Schleich takes this seriously, involving zoological experts to ensure their creations are as accurate as possible. This approach inevitably leads to higher prices, but the result is an animal that a child can really believe in, helping to make playtime more rewarding.

A wide range of accessories, including trees, buildings and human figurines, helps to add even more depth to the imaginative world of Schleich, but the fact is that many people do not even know they have a Schleich animal in the house. Sold loose, they are often given as presents to children who may never notice the small Schleich moulding on the underside of their new animal. Those children will, however, notice how lifelike their new animals are.

WATER PISTOL

www.hasbro.com

While we can't be sure when the first water pistol was invented, the *USA Liquid Pistol*, patented in 1896, is the earliest known example. Toy guns have received something of a bad press in recent years, but the water pistol has been mostly free from criticism (although they must be made to look like toys rather than accurate replicas, a fact that would render the *USA Liquid Pistol* unacceptable today).

The water pistol works on the time-honoured principle that throwing water at somebody is hilarious. A cup of water will do, even a handful if there is no receptacle available, but a water pistol, with its avowed purpose being to direct a targeted stream of water at your victim, is the only choice for anyone who takes their task seriously.

Following on from this basic principle is a secondary one. If throwing water at someone is amusing, then the more you throw at them, the more amusing it gets. The law of diminishing returns does not apply here.

With this in mind the water pistol has evolved steadily since 1896, with children now kitted out like special forces soldiers. *Blasters, Super Soakers* (invented by Lonnie Johnson in 1990) and *Saturators* all proudly boast of their water-hurling capabilities, with increasing power meaning that no corner of the garden is out of range. A sophisticated, technologically advanced answer to the primitive water balloon, the water pistol remains at the cutting edge of the backyard arms race.

ROLE-PLAY TOYS

MY LITTLE PONY

1983
Inventor: Bonnie Zacherle, Charles Muenchinger and Steven D. D'Aguanno
www.hasbro.com

Everyone knows that little girls love horses, so it's no surprise to see a second equine entry in our 100 classic toys, alongside the highly detailed Breyer models (see page 120). Unlike Breyer's horses, *My Little Pony* is firmly rooted in the fantasy world (if anything in the fantasy world can be firmly rooted).

The multi-coloured vinyl ponies arrived in 1983, with the first six characters – Cotton Candy, Blue Belle, Butterscotch, Minty, Snuzzle and Blossom – setting the stage for one cute release after another. Unicorns, ponies with rainbow manes and Pegasus ponies with fluttering wings all proved irresistible to little girls, leading to spin-off TV shows and movies.

The first generation of *MLP* ended in 1992 in the US (it continued for several years in other countries) and the G2 range, debuting in 1997, proved short-lived – the use of new poses and a harder plastic failing to impress the legion of expectant fans.

Further launches have been more successful. Today's ponies have been transformed into even 'cuter' styles, having bigger eyes and childlike faces, with seven characters at the heart of the range – Twilight Sparkle, Rainbow Dash, Fluttershy, Pinkie Pie, Applejack, Rarity and Princess Celestia.

My Little Pony is one of those toys that little girls never seem to grow out of, with many older girls still collecting them. For the most part, the boys remain unimpressed...

TRANSFORMERS

1984
Inventor: Nobuyuki Okude
www.transformers.com

As a key figure at Takara (now Tomy) in Japan, Nobuyuki Okude is credited with inventing the transforming robots that have been entertaining boys for almost three decades. Two Takara lines, 'Microman' and 'Diaclone', were combined under the terms of a partnership with Hasbro, who introduced the first *Transformers* toys to the US, Canada and the UK in 1984.

That's about as simple as the *Transformers* story gets. Since that 1984 launch (retrospectively known as *Transformers* Generation 1), characters have come and gone, taken part in conflicting storylines in print and onscreen and undergone countless re-designs. The line has also assimilated other film franchises to create new *Transformers* worlds.

At the heart of it all, however, is the engaging concept of toy robots that can be transformed by a child into other machines and even creatures. Cars, tanks, planes, fire engines – all have been used as the alter egos

of the *Transformers*, with the rich backstory adding depth to the gameplay.

The most familiar element is the struggle between the Autobots and the Decepticons, fulfilling the eternal roles of 'goodies' and 'baddies' with Optimus Prime and Megatron as the white-hat/black-hat duo at the heart of things.

Present in the original (and, die-hards would insist, best) G1 range of toys, Optimus Prime's and Megatron's battle recently spilled over onto the big screen, where the pair made it clear that the years have not mellowed them yet.

STRETCH ARMSTRONG

1976
Inventor: James O. Kuhn
www.stretcharmstrongworld.com

Few action figures take their job description as seriously as *Stretch Armstrong*. Stretch could be pulled into grotesque shapes, previously attainable only by victims of the Spanish Inquisition, and he would always slowly recover to his original shape, ready for more fun and games.

Stretch's secret wasn't really that exotic. Corn syrup, mixed to a certain consistency, has just the right properties to stretch and recover when encased in a rubber skin. The original US Patent application called for the doll to be 'in the shape of a muscular man or shapely woman' but, although many different variations on the theme have been tried, shapely women have never been part of the *Stretch Armstrong* world.

Stretch was tailor-made for TV advertising. Watch a 30-second advert and any child would know exactly what to expect from their flexible friend. Inevitably, kids would also be tempted to put *Stretch* to the test and see if they could pull his arms and legs off, but Stretch was mostly up to the challenge, and although tears could appear as the toy aged (or if fiendish instruments of torture were used on him, we're back to the Spanish Inquisition) he proved remarkably resilient.

The original patent outlined a giraffe version, but this also never appeared, although a *Stretch Monster* (looking very much like the creature from the black lagoon) soon arrived. Further variations included stretchy versions of the Hulk, a pair of *Stretch Octopuses* (Ollie and Olivia), an X-ray character with visible internal organs and a dog, called (quite brilliantly) *Fetch Armstrong*, while more recent variations on the theme have included the Power Rangers and Scooby-Doo.

Vintage Kenner *Stretch Armstrong* and *Stretch Monster*.

SYLVANIAN FAMILIES

1985
www.sylvanianfamilies.com

lthough it is tempting to consider *Sylvanian Families* as merely an elaborate offshoot of the dolls house (see page 124), it actually goes much further than this, creating an incredibly rich and detailed environment for children and adult collectors alike.

Introduced in 1985, and created by the Japanese company Epoch, the range is built on a collection of 'families' living in an idealised country setting (which has absolutely nothing to do with vampires). Where a dolls house creates a home, *Sylvanian Families* creates an entire world.

Elephants, otters, rabbits, cats and a vast number of other animal families live in harmony in Sylvania (you can move the Fisher Cat family in next door to the Barker Labradors with no fear of trouble), with an equally impressive

choice of dwellings. Windmills, hotels, restaurants and even hospitals have been created, with furniture sets available to keep the Sylvanians comfortable. The little critters can even go on holiday in a caravan.

With its emphasis on family life and gentle play, *Sylvanian Families* quickly generated a big following, especially among young girls, but after attaining craze proportions in the 1990s, the Sylvanian bubble was temporarily burst when falling sales sparked their withdrawal from the US and Canada (where they were known as *Calico Critters*) in 1996, with Britain following suit in 1998.

Thankfully, for Sylvanian lovers everywhere, this proved to be a brief hiatus, with distribution starting up again in 1999. Sylvania is back on the map.

STAR WARS ACTION FIGURES

1977
www.hasbro.com

*S*tar Wars Episode IV: A New Hope not only popularised surround sound and killed off a new TV series of *Star Trek*, it also spawned one of the most successful toy spin-off lines ever. The blasters had barely fallen silent before kids discovered miniature versions of their new onscreen heroes in toy shops around the world. The *Star Wars* action figures from Kenner were smaller than *G.I. Joe* (most of the figures were 3.75in. high), but they made up for that in numbers – you could get your hands on just about everyone from that galaxy far, far away.

The Kenner figures were never particularly impressive as examples of the action figure – articulation was severely limited – but boy, did they look the part, and although they could really only stand awkwardly and point their little plastic blasters at each other with dead straight arms, you could recreate all your favourite scenes from the most amazing movie you'd ever seen. The first wave of 12 figures launched in 1977 and was followed with regular updates, boosted every few years with a further instalment of the movie franchise.

Now produced by Hasbro, the figures have transformed into highly detailed, fully articulated figures covering characters from the movie series and the animated show *Star Wars: The Clone Wars*. They have been given toys of their own, a range of vehicles and spaceships, but although the new figures are undoubtedly far superior to their forebears, the original Kenner offerings have that irresistible retro appeal.

1977 Kenner Stormtrooper figure.

STYLING HEAD

1976
www.mattel.com

The styling head has been presented in many forms. Mattel blew up Barbie's head in 1976 to get the ball rolling, Palitoy launched *Girl's Word*, Mego brought us *Farrah's Glamour Center* (modelled on actress Farrah Fawcett) and there have been many more in the 40 or so years since.

Dolls tend to concentrate on outfits and role-play, while the styling head zooms in to focus on hair and make-up. Giving young girls a way to experiment with hair-styling and cosmetics application is undoubtedly a good idea – or, at least, a much better idea than letting them practice on a parent or younger sibling.

Some heads had 'growing' hair (really just a dial that could wind the hair in or out to vary its length – now why can't we have one of those?) and a supply of play make-up would be included, alongside plastic hairbrushes and curling tongs, but there was always the danger of little girls deciding to try mum's real make-up instead, or varying the hair length using more traditional, scissor-based techniques.

The idea has certainly proved (unlike the styling heads themselves) to have legs – today you can pick up any number of versions, including Disney Princesses, Dora the Explorer and Rapunzel. You can even get Barbie with her dog and an 'I Love Ponies' styling head from Vivid, which lets girls practice plaiting a mane while also allowing their brothers to recreate scenes from *The Godfather*.

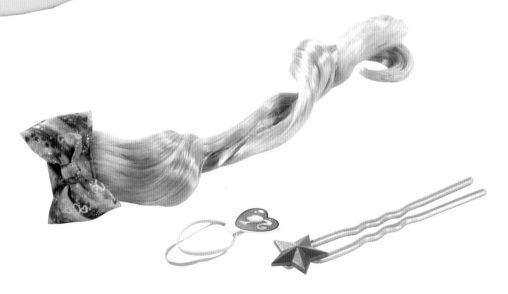

TEDDY BEARS
Steiff bear

1902
Inventor: Richard Steiff
www.steiff.com

Cuddly animals have been delighting children for centuries, but in 1902 a very special toy made its first appearance – and quickly clambered to the top of the pile. In fact, the Teddy bear has proved so successful, it's hard to imagine why it didn't appear sooner.

The first illustrated Steiff catalogue, produced in 1892, included a huge variety of animals, including monkeys, cats and horses, as well as less likely subjects such as pigs and camels. There were no bears. In fact, the company now most closely associated with the Teddy bear started out with a simple elephant pin cushion, designed by company founder Margarete Steiff. The elephant proved so popular with children, Margarete decided to market it as a toy, but it wasn't until 1902 that her nephew, Richard Steiff, designed the world's first bear with moveable arms and legs.

Margarete was not convinced, but an order from an American toy dealer (who took 3,000 copies of 'Bear 55PB' to the States to be sold as 'Teddy bears' in honour of President Theodore Roosevelt) put the Steiff bear on the map. It has stayed there ever since.

With a button sewn into one ear to guarantee authenticity, the Steiff bear has become synonymous with quality. The company still makes many other cuddly animals, but the bear, perhaps making up for arriving late, is the life and soul of the party.

TEDDY BEARS

1930
Inventor: Florence Atwood
www.merrythought.co.uk

In the UK, another long-lasting brand has fought back from the brink of closure to keep a tradition alive. The Merrythought traditional English mohair Teddy bear (to give it its full title) is nothing short of a national institution. Still producing hand-crafted bears in the same building the company started out in back in 1930, Merrythought is the only Teddy bear factory still operating in the UK.

1931 *Merrythought* Magnet Bear.

It was the introduction of synthetic fibres in the 1920s, and the subsequent fall in demand for mohair, that set the owners of a small Yorkshire spinning mill thinking about new ways to put their mohair yarn to use.

The solution became apparent when mill-owners W .G. Holmes and G. H. Laxton teamed up with a pair of toy industry veterans, A. C. Janisch and C. J. Rendle. No doubt pleased with their impressive collection of initials, the foursome settled down to produce soft toys, based at Coalbrookdale (now Ironbridge) in England.

It was then that the singular talents of Florence Atwood, as Merrythought's toy designer, came to the fore. Atwood (who, like Rendle, had previously been at Chad Valley) designed the entire 32-strong line for Merrythought's first year – and some of her patterns are still in use today.

Although the company originally offered a wide selection of different animals, stiff competition from other manufacturers pushed Merrythought to the brink of extinction. Production actually ceased briefly in 2006, but with a shift of focus to the classic Teddy bear, sought after by collectors and parents alike, the Merrythought flame was rekindled in 2007.

TOY SOLDIERS

The choice of the discerning schoolboy, toy soldiers have been thrilling youngsters for decades. Often criticised by pacifist groups (they are banned in some schools), their enduring appeal is impossible to crush — there's just something about a toy in uniform.

The secret to the global success of these little plastic men is that they appeal on so many different levels that almost every boy is caught in their net. Acquisitive types who want to build a complete collection and military enthusiasts who painstakingly paint their men in often exquisite detail can all find something to appeal.

Most boys, however, simply enjoy playing with their toy soldiers, and there is an endless list of scenarios to work through. The gallant last stand (I'm looking at you, 7th Cavalry), the dawn patrol, the last-minute rescue — all of these and more can be acted out using these 1:32 scale heroes.

Army men

www.thortrains.net/armymen/

The simplest versions, the 'army men' that achieved fame by appearing in the *Toy Story* films, are mass-produced figures, short on detail but long on playability. With a history that has embraced warriors from just about every major conflict and many countries, the American G.I. of the mid-20th century remains the standard bearer of this range. Although produced in various colours to signify different nationalities, the dark green (roughly matching the colour worn by the American soldier in World War II) is most famous.

These basic toy soldiers have been produced by many companies, notably Louis Marx in America, and include cheaper imitations from the Far East. Cheapness is, in fact, one of the defining qualities of these expendable plastic soldiers, which are designed to be sold in bags, or even buckets, at a low price.

1970s World War II *Airfix* soldiers.

Airfix 1:32 soldiers

www.airfix.com

More detailed versions came from Airfix in the form of the company's *Military Series* soldiers. Sold in beautifully illustrated boxes (the distinctive circular motif on each box led to them being referred to as 'target' boxes), these men were of a different class altogether. Carefully sculpted, with a surprising amount of detail, Airfix's soldiers were designed to be played with or painted and attracted adult collectors, as well as schoolboys.

One similarity with the cheaper army men was the use of colour coding for the troops of different nations. Airfix's American WWII soldiers were also moulded from a dark green plastic, with dark grey for the Germans, light tan for the British Eighth Army (they spent a lot of time in the sun, after all) and so on. Quirkily, the sizes of each nation's soldiers were slightly different, although all officially 1:32 scale. The German Infantry figures, for instance, were far bulkier than their counterparts from other nations. Original target-boxed Airfix

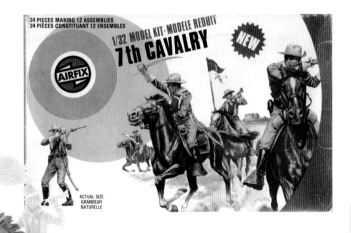

1974 Indians and 1975
7th Cavalry *Airfix* soldiers.

William Britain Super Deetail

www.wbritain.comwww.airfix.com

soldiers change hands for as much as £50 a box on internet sites, and there was huge excitement in 2009 when Airfix relaunched several ranges. With re-designed boxes (sadly without that iconic target motif), the soldiers are also modelled from a harder plastic, which aids painting but makes delicate sections like gun barrels more brittle.

The third standout entry in this crowded field is the 1:32 scale men from William Britain (also known as Britains). Originally a producer of lead soldiers (the company pioneered the technique of hollow casting in 1893, allowing its soldiers to be more affordable than those of its rivals), its emphasis shifted as plastic soldiers began to appear. Britains bought out a manufacturer of plastic soldiers, Herald, in 1959, and plastic soldiers then became the main focus, with

production of hollowcast metal figures ceasing in 1966.

With a portfolio of figures including ancient Greek warriors, cowboys and Indians and U.S. cavalry, Britains' plastic soldiers were not as heavily detailed as their Airfix rivals, but they had one key advantage — they came ready-painted.

The painting was fairly basic but extremely effective and Britains figures added a dash of colour to miniature battlefields all over the world. The painting process inevitably added to the price of these soldiers, which were sold individually rather than in boxes, allowing them to remain pocket-money friendly.

Britains still produces a wide range of plastic soldiers in the Super Deetail Plastics line and the company's metal soldiers are back on active duty as well, now aimed squarely at the collectors market.

1970s *William Britain* soldiers.

William Britain American mortar set.

5 Trucks and transport

CARS
Matchbox

1953
Inventor: Jack Odell
www.matchbox.com

If any toy can lay claim to rivalling toy soldiers in the affections of young boys around the world, the die-cast car is it. Shrinking real cars down to micro size appeals across a broad spectrum, calling out to neophyte petrol heads, wannabe racing drivers, budding collectors and any boy who just dreams of owning his own car. That covers an awful lot of little boys.

The name that has become almost synonymous with die-cast cars, *Matchbox*, is so perfect that it's difficult to see how anyone else got a look in. For a while, nobody else did. Lesney, the company set up by Leslie Smith and Rodney Smith (no relation, to me or to each other), had been making die-cast metal vehicles since 1948, but it was the *Diesel Road Roller* of 1953 that was the first to be shrunk to matchbox proportions.

Matchbox lore says that it was Lesney partner Jack Odell's daughter who provided the spark for the move to miniature size. Her school insisted that all show-and-tell items be small enough to fit into a matchbox, so Odell make an extra small version of the company's existing *Road Roller* (delighting his daughter and making all other dads feel inadequate at the same time). The tiny vehicles proved so popular that Lesney had phased out production of larger models within a year.

Enjoying success out of all proportion to the size of its products, *Matchbox* hit cruise control, unaware that a major roadblock was being assembled ahead. Mattel was designing a new range of toy cars on the same scale as those from *Matchbox*.

Matchbox Models of Yesteryear B-Type Bus.

CARS
Hot Wheels

1968
Inventor: Elliott Handler
www.hotwheels.com

Elliott Handler (husband of Barbie-creator Ruth and co-founder of Mattel, making the Handlers the undisputed dream ticket of the toy world) had been tinkering with the idea of a range of miniature cars to rival those of *Matchbox*. Realising that differentiation would be important, he designed cars with low-friction wheels and working suspension, which ran much more smoothly and quickly than their British counterparts, and called them *Hot Wheels*.

Hot Wheels also concentrated on the most desirable cars available in America – including the Firebird, Mustang, Camaro and Barracuda – with eye-catching paint jobs. A total of 16 *Hot Wheels* purred off the production line in 1968 and parked themselves on the wish-lists of kids everywhere.

Lesney saw the writing on the wall (and the downward angle of its sales chart was equally easy to read) and quickly responded with its *Superfast* range, reclaiming *Matchbox*'s position as a major player in the die-cast world and possibly saving the company from extinction. The two brands would remain rivals until 1997, when Mattel bought Tyco, which had bought *Matchbox* in 1992.

1969 *Hot Wheels* Twin Mill.

CARS
Corgi

1956
www.corgi.co.uk

Sitting neatly between the launch dates of *Matchbox* and *Hot Wheels*, *Corgi* offered something different. Windows. Having plastic windows on toy cars is standard now but, back in 1956, *Corgi* was the first company to offer it, and *Corgi* cars were marketed, and became known as, 'the ones with windows'. It may seem like a small thing, and it's certainly a more humble slogan than we're used to in today's marketing, but differences count, and the windows were only symptomatic of an overall approach to detail that caught the eye of car enthusiasts – glinting headlights and opening doors, bonnets and boots would follow.

Corgi has released thousands of models, debuting with British saloon cars including the Morris Cowley,

Riley Pathfinder and Hillman Husky — names guaranteed to make a car buff misty-eyed – but the company is best known for its movie and TV tie-ins. The 1965 James Bond Aston Martin DB5 sold almost four million

Corgi Aston Martin DB5.

units in its first three years alone (in this case, having windows probably took second billing to having front-mounted machine guns and an ejector seat), while the 1966 Batmobile topped the five million mark.

Corgi started out as Mettoy in 1934 and was briefly owned by Mattel (from 1989 to 1995), but is now part of the Hornby group, giving it the prestigious stablemates (and fellow subjects in this book) of Airfix, Scalextric and Hornby.

Although Mattel produces a range of playsets and racetracks for its die-cast cars, *Corgis* are strictly standalone vehicles, but even the *Matchbox* and *Hot Wheels* accessories are really nothing compared with the world created for the final entry in our classic toy cars section.

CARS
Tomica

1970
www.tomica-usa.com

Original *Tomica* line-up.

In Japan, little metal cars have been part of an engrossing and stunningly diverse world for over 40 years. The *Tomica* range started in 1970 with the release of six die-cast cars. Originally concentrating on domestic vehicles, the first offerings were the Bluebird SSS Coupe, the Corona Mark II 1900, the Crown Super Deluxe, the Crown Patrol Car, the Toyota 2000GT and the Nissan Fairlady Z432. The cars were actually produced in slightly different scales, ranging from 1:60 to 1:65.

Initial attempts to export the *Tomica* line were unsuccessful due to the Japanese-only offerings, so foreign makes were included from 1976 onwards. Although the *Tomica* name has endured, it is the simple, traditional cars that have carried the brand. Military, motorised and pullback versions have all been tried and discarded, while the simple die-casts roll on.

Tomica also embraces a wealth of accessories. From petrol stations to pizza parlours, roads and car parks, enthusiasts can build a highly detailed town or city for their little toy cars to drive around in. In 2010, the *Tomica* line was launched in the UK and America, merged with the *Plarail* train system (see page 178) to form a fully integrated world based on the concept of the modern urban environment. In the *Tomica HyperCity*, die-cast cars can rub shoulders with high-speed bullet trains and rescue vehicles – and we're sure they won't mind if you bring your *Matchbox*, *Corgi* and *Hot Wheels* cars along too.

COZY COUPE

1979
www.littletikes.com

O ver more than three decades, the *Cozy Coupe* has given millions of children that first special taste of freedom that can only come with ownership of a car – a red and yellow plastic car, yes, but a car nonetheless.

The *Cozy Coupe*, from Little Tikes, launched in 1979 and over 20 million have been sold so far. In 2008, in fact, the *Cozy Coupe* was the best-selling car in America.

The appeal of this car is obvious – you drive it in the same way that Fred Flintstone drives his, by sticking your feet out of the bottom and running. Fred's frankly old-fashioned car is, however, made of rocks and tree trunks, so the *Cozy Coupe* is streets ahead in terms of handling.

There's also no need to wait until you are 16 or 17, your own car is within reach from the age of 18 months, and Little Tikes added a few new wrinkles for the Coupe's 30th anniversary, making it an even more desirable run-around.

The *Cozy Coupe* always had realistic features like an ignition switch, an open-and-close petrol tank cover and as many gears as a child's little legs had in them. The 30th

anniversary edition added an improved seat and (addressing a need sadly ignored by other car manufacturers) a big smiley cartoon face at the front.

Experts have estimated that kids will burn up 33 calories in every 20 minutes of playing in a *Cozy Coupe*. They'd probably burn up much more just running around, but that's cars for you.

Original *Cozy Coupe*.

BIG TRAK

1979
www.bigtrakisback.com

*B*IG TRAK (or *bigtrak*, as it was known in the UK) was a programmable robotic tank that was firmly at the cutting edge of electronic toy design when it came out in 1979. Despite technology having moved on at a scorching pace, making *BIG TRAK* look positively Stone Age compared with modern gizmos, it retains a huge appeal and was recently relaunched in both full- and half-sized versions.

The initial appeal of *BIG TRAK* stemmed from its awesome sci-fi design, guaranteed to get young kids' jaws dropping – the toy would probably have been a success as a simple .

push-along vehicle for use with a space-age action figure, but *BIG TRAK* offered far more than that.

Actually, if truth be told, it wasn't exactly 'far more', just a bit more. You could program *BIG TRAK* to move and turn, but there was only capacity in its tiny memory for 16 commands. Funnily enough, at the dawn of the 1980s' technology explosion, that seemed more than adequate, especially when one of the commands offered was a defiant blast from *BIG TRAK*'s photon cannon.

Some of the instructions now seem wonderfully quaint — 'Telling *BIG TRAK*'s computer what to do is called "programming"... To "program" *BIG TRAK*, you enter instructions into the keypad...'. You can almost imagine Dr. Evil explaining this, complete with air quotes, in an Austin Powers movie.

But that's enough levity. *BIG TRAK* offered six wheels of fun in a more innocent time and heralded a new era in children's entertainment. The electronics age had begun, and we loved it.

SCALEXTRIC

1957
Inventor: Bertram Francis
www.scalextric.com

Bertram 'Fred' Francis was already successfully producing clockwork, tinplate 'Scalex' racing cars when he hit on the idea of adding a small electric motor to each vehicle to liven things up a bit. Duly enlivened (and with a corresponding adjustment to the product's name), the new *Scalextric* was launched in 1957 at the Harrogate Toy Fair in the UK, with a set featuring a pair of 1:32 scale Maserati 250Fs.

The basic principles of the system have endured over the ensuing half century, although the 'gimbal' electric pickup (a fifth wheel situated between and just behind the front pair) was quickly replaced with the more familiar brush plates, and tinplate gave way to plastic in 1960.

In 2004, a major step was taken with the introduction of new digital sets, which made it possible to race six individually controlled cars on a two-lane track and even allowed for overtaking. Cars have also got faster, with customised models now reaching scale speeds approaching 1,000mph.

The proliferation of *Scalextric* sets has seen motorbikes and sidecars, lorries, skateboards (ridden by Teenage Mutant Ninja Turtles, no less) and even horses shrunk down to scoot around that familiar slotted track, but it's the cars that *Scalextric* is famous for.

Fred wasn't around to see his creation develop, however. It turned out that cars weren't his main passion in life and he sold his Minimodels company in 1958, just one year after launching *Scalextric*, so that he could devote his time to his really serious interests — flying and sailing.

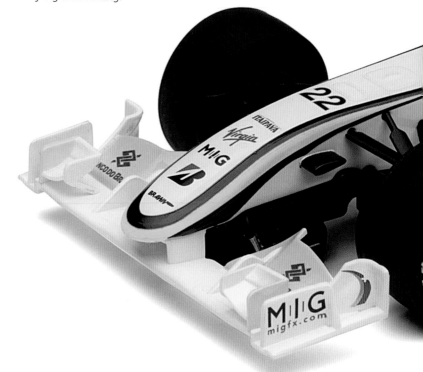

Maserati 250F – the first car.

TONKA

1947
www.hasbro.com

When a job needs doing, you need the right tools. When it comes to really serious play, you need a really serious toy. *Tonka* built its reputation by making insanely tough toys, able to mimic the jobs of their real-life counterparts in backyards throughout the world. Emerging from Mound Metalcraft and named after Lake Minnetonka, *Tonka* took a while to grow into its name ('Tonka' means 'great' in the Sioux language), but with the arrival of Russ Wenkstern in 1952, the range of products grew and the manufacturing process became more robust. In 1995 the company was renamed Tonka Toys, Inc.

Interestingly, *Tonka* avoided making direct replicas of existing vehicles, preferring to cherry pick the best qualities from a range of sources and combine them to make an idealised version. Even so, made from steel, using cutting-edge progressive tooling, *Tonka*'s products felt 'real'. The scale was enormous, at 1:18, making sure that when a *Tonka* toy was under the tree on Christmas morning, you knew about it.

From 1964, the one most hankered-after was the legendary *Mighty Tonka Dump Truck*, a yellow behemoth so tough a child could ride on it. Adverts of the day talked of the 'Tonka touch', and everyone knew exactly what that meant.

Tonka had earned its name and although some of today's versions have switched to cheaper plastic, the name remains evocative of an era when, for just a few glorious decades, a child's toy was almost as tough as the real thing.

1961 *Tonka* Dump Truck.

TRAINS
Lionel Trains

1902
Inventor: Joshua Lionel Cowen
www.lionel.com

Baffling as it may seem to some, many children dream of one day becoming a train driver, or at least having a go at driving a locomotive. It was love at first sight when trains first started puffing their way across the countryside in the first half of the 19th century, and the first toy trains followed almost instantly.

Early examples were push-along models where children supplied the power themselves, but by the end of the century, battery-powered trains were appearing and in 1902 Joshua Lionel Cowen saw the potential of supplying a toy train that ran on electric power along a scale track. *Lionel* trains were a hit from the start, and a post-World War II sales boom, and the concurrent population explosion in America, saw the company reach its zenith.

Lionel was most notable for its O gauge sets, offering trains in 1:48 scale that ran on a three-rail track system. The large locomotives that the O gauge scale created were able to carry a tremendous amount of detail, helping to appeal to fathers as well as sons (a 1957 set aimed specifically at girls, with pink and pastel engines and cars, failed to win over the fairer sex).

Living large was also *Lionel*'s downfall, with increasing competition from smaller-gauge competitors among the factors that led to the company declaring itself bankrupt in 1967. The brand endured, however (despite a procession of ownership changes), and *Lionel Trains* are now produced by Lionel, LLC, with O gauge firmly at the top of the pecking order.

1925 *Lionel* Trains brochure.

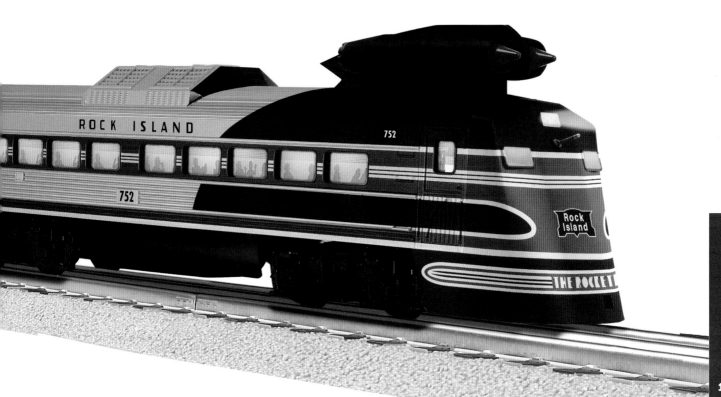

TRAINS
Hornby

1920
Inventor: Frank Hornby
www.hornby.com

At the same time that Lionel was wowing Americans, *Hornby* was making an impact in Britain on a smaller scale – OO gauge, which is roughly half the size of *Lionel*'s O gauge. *Hornby* had dabbled with the larger scale for its first trains, but by 1938 the first OO gauge (known as *Hornby Dublo*) trains arrived, an LNER A4 Class Pacific and an LNER Class N2 tank locomotive, each in a choice of four liveries.

Hornby enjoyed a post-war boom too, but there were also less welcome parallels with *Lionel* as company ownership changed several times.

Hornby's appeal lay in the ability to create satisfyingly complex layouts in limited space, taking into account the constraints of the average British home. Trains were the stars, but the supporting cast of scenery, buildings and miniature people provided the backdrop that made them shine.

Both *Lionel* and *Hornby* sets are also able to appeal to multiple generations at the same time, a rare achievement for a toy. Children, parents and grandparents can look at the same layout and each get something rewarding, yet different, from it. The child might dream of one day being a train driver, the parent might relish the technical challenge of organising an efficient rail service, while the grandparent might remember receiving the first part of the layout as a child.

TRAINS
BRIO

1957
Inventors: Victor, Anton, and Emil Ivarsson
www.brio.net

In stark contrast to the realistic models of the *Lionel* and *Hornby* worlds, BRIO approaches toy trains from a completely different direction. Wooden trains and tracks aimed at young children might draw a nostalgic smile from a parent, but are less likely to tempt them to get involved beyond the initial setting-up of a layout.

BRIO's trains are, for the most part, unpowered (there are battery-powered trains with light and sound effects, but the standard sets use push-along models) and it is arguable that the wooden tracks are one of the few toys to improve with age, becoming smoother and gaining character over the years.

Fitting the tracks together into a working circuit offers a gentle challenge for young minds, making BRIO trains a developmental toy (not that the kids realise this), but you are less likely to see an enormous, room-filling *BRIO* layout of the kind *Lionel* and *Hornby* encourage. You can get ambitious with the use of switchable points and sidings, but *BRIO* is mostly intended to be easy to set up and easy to clear away after play.

High production values appeal to parents, who see wooden toys as somehow more 'real' than modern electronic wizardry, allowing *BRIO* to set eyebrow-raising prices, but, as the old saying goes, you get what you pay for.

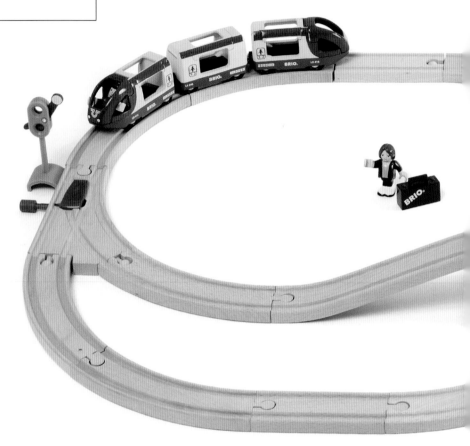

TRUCKS AND TRANSPORT

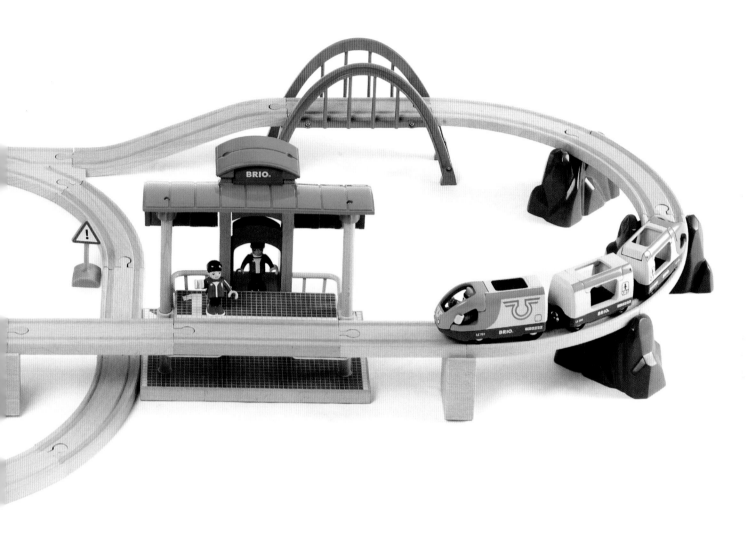

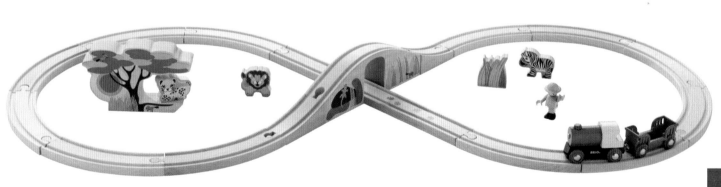

TRAINS
Plarail

1959
www.tomy.com

*P*larail, from Tomy, represents yet another approach to the world of toy trains. Launched in Japan in 1959, *Plarail* uses distinctive blue plastic track and is part of the *Tomica World* play system. The use of plastic was innovative at the time and battery-powered trains were added in 1961.

Plarail, like *Hornby* and *Lionel*, also has a devoted adult following. This is partly due to the vast selection of accessories available, including buildings and figures, which allow for extremely intricate layouts. The way Plarail dovetails with the Tomica toy cars brand (see page 165) adds to the possibilities.

Perhaps most important, however, is the way Plarail bridges the gap between the 'serious' trains of Hornby and Lionel and the play trains of BRIO. Plarail offers a huge selection of locomotives and carriages, including many of the famous Japanese 'bullet trains', guaranteed to call out to train enthusiasts of all ages. Delving into the world of Thomas the Tank Engine, also adds appeal to a range that only recently ventured beyond the shores of Japan.

Early *Plarail* train.

TRUCKS AND TRANSPORT

6 Toys for making things

PLAY-DOH

1955
Inventors: Joe and N.W. McVicker
www.hasbro.com

Vintage *Play-Doh* tub.

The story of *Play-Doh* is almost the exact opposite of that of *Silly Putty* (see page 187). Both are squidgy compounds that kids love to get their hands on, but while Silly Putty emerged as a toy only after a fruitless quest to find some useful application for it, *Play-Doh* had existed as a very useful household cleaning material for over 20 years before someone realised it could be made into a toy.

Starting life as *Kutol Wall Cleaner*, with a knack for removing dirt from wallpaper, *Play-Doh* emerged 22 years later only slightly changed. Some chemicals were removed, but the most important change was the addition of a new scent, the *Play-Doh* aroma that can whisk an adult back to those halcyon nursery days with a single sniff.

Play-Doh was originally sold in big tubs intended for schools, in an off-white colour. Red, blue and yellow followed quickly and the colours have kept coming over the years. The tubs have become smaller as *Play-Doh* has been embraced all over the world, while fun factories, shape cutters and even barber shops have all been created to squeeze as much fun as possible from the multi-coloured stuff.

Over two billion tubs of *Play-Doh* have been sold worldwide and it also provides a valuable lesson in the difference between smell and taste, as every curious toddler has discovered when taking a nibble of that delicious-smelling compound.

AIRFIX

1952
www.airfix.com

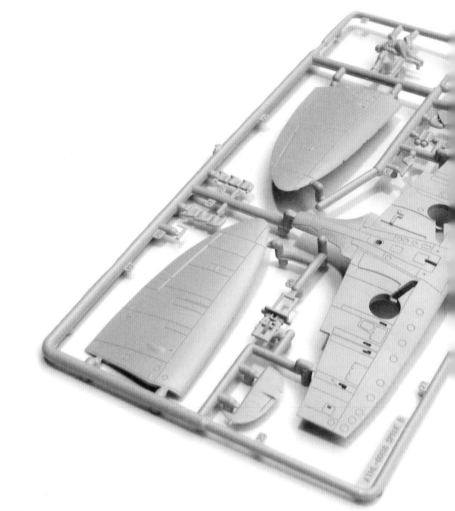

For more than 60 years children (mostly boys) and their parents (mostly fathers) have been gluing small plastic pieces together to produce models of aircraft, ships, military vehicles and cars. The fact that ready-made models of all of these can be easily found in toy shops around the world is proof that when it comes to *Airfix*, the journey is more important than the destination.

It's a bit of a surprise, therefore, to realise that the journey was not planned. The first plastic model produced by *Airfix*, in 1949, was of a Ferguson tractor – and it was nothing more than a promotional item for Ferguson's salespeople. Finding that it was difficult to fix the pieces of the tractor together well enough for it to stand up to the rigours of being shipped out to the Ferguson offices, the people at *Airfix* hit on a masterstroke. They sent the kit out in pieces, for the staff at Ferguson to put together themselves.

Cottoning on to this intriguing concept, *Airfix* started to sell models of the tractor to the public and in 1952 the first specially produced kit aimed squarely at the public was released, a 1:72 scale model of the *Golden Hind*.

Despite the *Golden Hind* launching first, the *Spitfire* remains the darling of *Airfix* and its legion of fans. A vast range of *Spitfire* models has been released since the first, the Mk 1, in 1953, and the *Spitfire* still retains pride of place in the current *Airfix* range, tempting a new generation of children to pick up a tube of glue and get to work.

1952 Golden Hind.

ETCH A SKETCH

1960
Inventor: Arthur Grandjean
www.flairplc.co.uk

The *Etch a Sketch* is the duck of the toy world. On the surface all is calm and serene as you etch out your masterpiece on the glass screen. Underneath that screen, it's all action as a sophisticated system of steel wires, pulleys, bars and aluminium powder translate your instructions, delivered via two control knobs, into art.

Few toys have intrigued children as much as the *Etch a Sketch*. Since its launch in 1960, the familiar red plastic box has posed two fundamental questions.

1 – How does it work? Watch a child with an *Etch a Sketch* and before long he or she will stop creating pictures and start to methodically erase the silver coating on the interior of the screen in an attempt to find out what's inside.

2 — Exactly how good can an *Etch a Sketch* picture be? Early efforts will involve nothing more ambitious than an attempt to draw an accurate square. Soon the goal will be a diagonal line and finally you might even attempt to draw a convincing curve. Some people progress to the stage where they can produce stunningly detailed pictures — a bit of a concern when turning the *Etch a Sketch* upside down will instantly erase all that hard work.

The secret to the *Etch a Sketch* is, of course, that aluminium powder, which sticks to anything it touches, including glass. The control knobs, working on vertical and horizontal axes, guide a stylus, which scrapes off the powder to reveal a line thanks to the dark interior of the *Etch a Sketch* casing.

Thankfully, as proved by decades of success, this is one magic trick that doesn't lose its appeal once you know how it works.

SILLY PUTTY

1950
Inventor: James Wright
www.sillyputty.com

If scientists had been able to find a single practical application for *Silly Putty*, it might never have become a toy at all. Invented by Scottish engineer James Wright during the Second World War, *Silly Putty* was an attempt to discover a synthetic replacement for natural rubber, which was scarce due to Japanese encroachment on rubber-producing countries in the Far East.

By mixing boric acid and silicone oil, Wright made a substance that was part liquid and part solid – and which bounced when thrown against a hard surface. Surely this amazing substance could be put to some use?

Luckily for us, despite everyone's best efforts, absolutely no application could be found and the pointless compound was about to quietly disappear when an American toy shop owner, Ruth Fallgatter, had the idea to sell it as a toy. In 1950, marketing consultant Peter Hodgson coined the perfect name for this most impractical substance, and *Silly Putty* was officially born.

The story might still have ended there if high-brow magazine *The New Yorker* hadn't published an article on it, triggering an avalanche of orders – but the market was initially made up mainly of adults (after all, how many kids read *The New Yorker*?), who saw it as a fun novelty, and it took five years for kids to take over as the main users.

Over 300 million egg-shaped cases of *Silly Putty* have now been sold. It has accompanied Apollo 8 astronauts to the moon, earned a place in America's Smithsonian Museum and spawned several similar toys. Not bad for a product with no practical use.

FUZZY-FELT

1950
Inventor: Lois Allan
www.johnadams.co.uk

It's strange to think that such a gentle toy as *Fuzzy-Felt* was developed from military technology – well, sort of. During World War II, the use of felt gaskets in tank parts resulted in lots of little off-cuts, which the factory workers' children soon realised could be used for play. They were especially effective when stuck to the back of table mats (which often had a fuzzy backing that the felt pieces stuck to readily).

Lois Allan, who was involved in the production of these felt gaskets at the family cottage in Buckinghamshire, realised that there was potential for a successful toy here and, in 1950, she marketed the first *Fuzzy-Felt* sets, sold through John Lewis and Heals.

Fuzzy-Felt was a big hit ('They cling like magic on the fuzzy board!') and many themed sets were soon boosting sales, which topped a million per year in the toy's 1970s heyday. Simplicity, as is so often the case with classic toys, was key – children could quickly and easily make effective scenes regardless of their artistic ability, while the more creative types would be happily occupied creating more complicated patterns.

Although the *Play-Farm Set* is undoubtedly the most famous *Fuzzy-Felt* incarnation (and one that can reduce many an adult to a state of dreamy-eyed nostalgia), the range has become ever more diverse over the years and now includes such licenses as *Thomas the Tank Engine*, *In the Night Garden* and *Timmy Time*.

Although sales have inevitably dipped over the past few decades, this is one toy that is still guaranteed to give children and grown-ups a warm, fuzzy feeling. Literally.

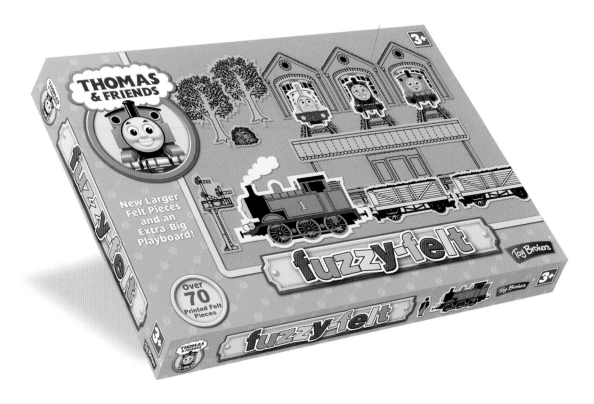

Traditional
fuzzy ® felt
Since 1950
Sealife

age
3-6

Put them on - take them off - they cling like magic on the fuzzy board

Traditional
fuzzy ® felt
Since 1950
Hospital

...them on - take them off - they cling like magic on the fuzzy board

Traditional
fuzzy ® felt
Since 1950
Ballet

age
3-6

Put them on - take them off - they cling like magic on the fuzzy board

TOYS FOR MAKING THINGS

PLASTICINE

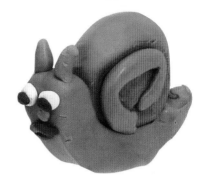

1897
Inventor: William Harbutt
www.flairplc.co.uk

alcium salts, petroleum jelly and aliphatic acids don't sound like much fun, and on their own they probably aren't. Mix them in the right way, however, and you get the most famous modelling compound of them all.

Plasticine was invented by William Harbutt in 1897. Initially it was a dull grey, but perhaps realising that this would be a hard sell, the first packs offered to the public featured four colours.

The main strength of *Plasticine* is that it does not dry out when left exposed to air. This not only means that kids can leave models out overnight and continue to work on them the next day, it also made it possible for a legion of *Plasticine* characters like Morph, Wallace and Gromit to remain flexible during the laborious production process of stop-motion animated films.

Plasticine was nearly lost when a series of ownership changes saw it disappear from the shops in the 1980s, but in 2005 Flair Leisure relaunched the brand and it is once more firmly established as a classic.

Available in a rainbow of hues, different colours can be mixed together — although as any child will tell you, go too far and you're left with nothing more than a muddy brown, with all the appeal of the original grey.

SPIROGRAPH

1965
Inventor: Denys Fisher
www.hasbro.com

It looks like something from a geometry set, requires complicated mathematical formulae to explain and produces curves known as hypotrochoids and epitrochoids – so how can the *Spirograph* possibly be a toy, let alone one that has been popular for generations?

The answer is simple. It produces pretty patterns.

The *Spirograph*, invented by British engineer Denys Fisher (who was inspired after hearing patterns in Beethoven's *Ninth Symphony*), was first demonstrated at the 1965 Nuremberg International Toy Fair and appears to produce pretty patterns out of nowhere. Arthur C. Clarke once famously stated that any sufficiently advanced technology is indistinguishable from magic, and as far as kids are concerned the *Spirograph* is magic.

Insert one *Spirograph* section (a 'rotor') inside another (a 'stator'), press a pen through a small hole onto a piece of paper and start to move the interior section within the exterior section. The teeth on both pieces will engage like gears, producing smooth curves and slowly building up a complex geometric pattern on the paper. The longer you keep at it, the more complex and beautiful the design will become. Use different coloured pens and the results can be psychedelic.

With the decades bringing us 3D, magnetic and foil versions, as well as options for younger children (the charmingly named *Spirotot*), *Spirograph* is undoubtedly the most successful toy that you need a degree in mathematics to fully comprehend.

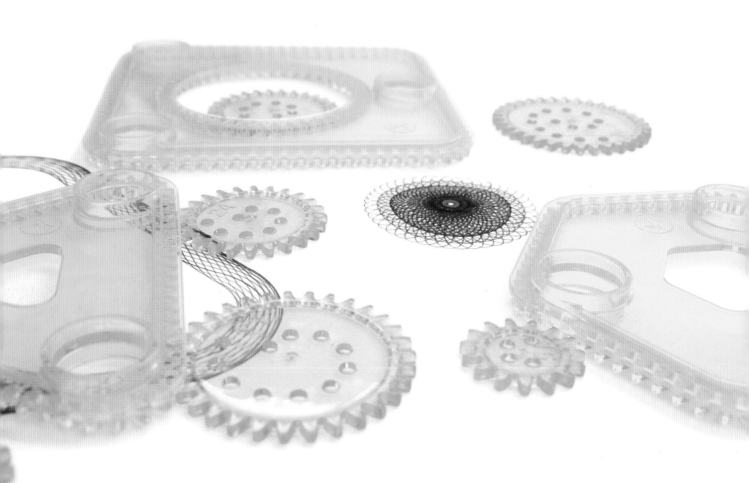

SHAKER MAKER

1971
www.flairplc.co.uk

Small, unpainted figures might attract a niche following among children, especially with the added power of licensing bringing popular characters from TV and the movies into the equation, but they probably wouldn't become classic toys.

Let the children make the figures themselves prior to painting and the appeal instantly goes up a notch or two. Throw in the irresistible gimmick of shaking the mould to create those figures and what you've got is a hit.

The very name *Shaker Maker* is proof of where the appeal of this toy lies. It isn't in the small figures that are the end product of the process – it is firmly rooted in the shaking and the making. By pouring 'Magic Mix' into the provided moulds, kids can create a carefully sculpted work of art with the application of no more skill than that needed to vigorously shake the mould (inadvertently creating a generation of children with a vague desire to work in cocktail bars).

Actually, there is at least a little skill involved – an imperfect technique might lead to the mould not filling correctly, and getting the 'Magic Mix' wrong in the first place might lead to it failing to set – but for the most part this is a simple but enjoyable process and many children don't even bother painting the figures after they have finally set solid (shrinking significantly in the process). They are already shaking and making more figures.

7 Future classics

AUTOMOBLOX
K'NEX
BUZZ LIGHTYEAR
GEOMAG

and finally...
THE CARDBOARD BOX

AUTOMOBLOX

2004
Inventor: Patrick Calello
www.automoblox.com

A good idea isn't enough when it comes to creating and marketing a classic toy. Patrick Calello found it easy enough to dream up the *Automoblox* concept – he did this while still studying graphic design at Carnegie Mellon University – but that was in 1992. It would be 2004 before *Automoblox* reached the market.

In the intervening 12 years, Calello graduated, juggled the development of his wooden cars with full-time jobs and learned invaluable lessons about marketing, production, research and branding. There were also painful lessons about manufacturing in China, which nearly derailed the entire project, but in 2004 the first *Automoblox* cars went on sale.

Automoblox is marketed as a modern heirloom toy,

intentionally designed to be handed from one generation to the next. To achieve this the cars must be durable and have a unique appeal.

Durability is taken care of by the use of renewable beech wood and polycarbonate plastic (the cars can support a weight of 50kg), while the unique appeal comes with the clever modular construction system, which means that children can completely dismantle the car (even the tyres come off) and enjoy putting it back together again. If two or more *Automoblox* cars are available, kids can even get creative and build their own hybrid vehicles..

It adds up to an elegant fusion of modern design and retro styling, making *Automoblox* a solid bet to one day stake a place in the pantheon of classic toys.

K'NEX

1992
Inventor: Joel Glickman
www.knex.com

A lot of things can go through your mind while sitting at a wedding reception. How long are these speeches going to last? What exactly was that dessert? Why didn't she marry me?

Joel Glickman put his time to much better use when he became intrigued with a straw at a busy wedding reception. Wondering what he might be able to create if there was a way to join straws together, he realised that he had stumbled upon an idea for a new construction toy. Those wedding day musings resulted in the launch of *K'Nex*, in 1992.

Rejected by the major toy companies, Glickman persevered and brought the new toy out himself. *K'Nex* works on a simple rod-and-connector principle, similar in some ways to *Tinkertoy* (see page 15), but Glickman soon added extra elements to improve the toy's capabilities. Gears, pulleys and wheels add to the range of construction possibilities and the addition of motors means that *K'Nex* models can now move.

In fact, they can do much more than that. You can build a Ferris wheel that lights up and a rollercoaster with a built-in video camera for producing hair-raising home movies. With *K'Nex* sets offering multiple builds, as well as the option of simply inventing something yourself, the company's three-word slogan really does encapsulate the brand perfectly.

Imagine. Build. Play.

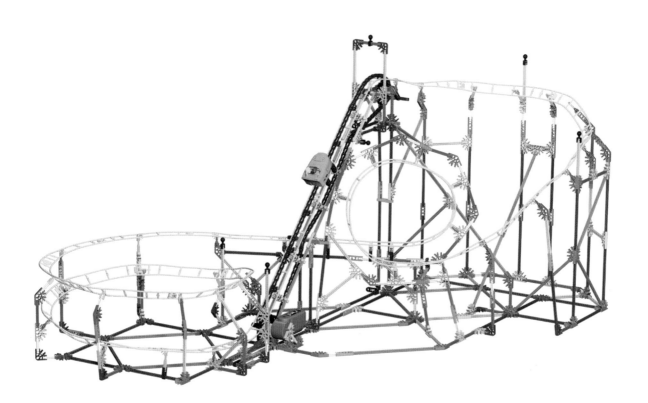

BUZZ LIGHTYEAR

1995
www.thinkwaytoys.com

With most action figures, a child needs to add the belief, imagining that it really is a soldier or robot or other heroic type. With Thinkway Toy's *Buzz Lightyear* action figure, the child is not alone. Buzz is right there with them.

Buzz, as anyone who's seen the *Toy Story* movies knows, actually believes he is a Space Ranger. Okay, the *Buzz Lightyear* that finds its way into Andy's House wises up after a few misadventures, but every other *Buzz Lightyear*, including the one your child owns, is still convinced that his laser actually works and that the evil Emperor Zurg could be around the next corner, still building that dastardly planet-destroying weapon that sounds suspiciously like the Death Star. Hitching a ride on a 2008 Space Shuttle

mission no doubt added to Buzz's conviction.

Buzz is a brilliant character to base an action figure on. His comically self-important attitude, all-American smile (which stops just short of smugness) and can-do approach make him instantly loveable, while he comes with the sort of gadgets and gizmos that any action figure would kill for – retractable wings, an opening helmet, built-in laser...

Thinkway Toys also produced a deluxe version of Buzz, with 65 built-in phrases (supplied by actor Tim Allen), spaceship packaging and light-up wingtips. Having been around for 16 years, Buzz is already on the brink of attaining classic status and his appeal will surely endure. As Woody declares in *Toy Story*: 'You! Are! A! Toy!'

We couldn't agree more.

GEOMAG

1998
www.geomagworld.com

The plastic rods and metal spheres of the *Geomag* construction system allow you to build almost any shape you like, resulting in one of the most satisfying hands-on toys out there. The tactile nature of *Geomag*, and the way the magnets at the end of each connecting rod grab the metal spheres, make building with *Geomag* an absorbing process.

It's also a process that can teach kids an awful lot about structures and construction principles – in fact, *Geomag* was lauded as one of the best educational toys available by *Scientific American* magazine, with a Harvard University lecturer praising it for its didactic qualities. Fan sites showcase complex structures like the cuboctahedron and rhombicosidodeca-hedron, whatever they are.

If all that sounds a bit too serious, you may be relieved to know that *Geomag* introduced a new 'KIDS' rod in 2009, longer and suitable for younger children to play with, and even babies can now get in on the fun with a Gbaby line-up. The original *Geomag*, now named *Geomag Pro*, is no longer marketed as a toy, yet it retains appeal for young and old alike. The brand continues to evolve, with 2011 seeing the introduction of *Geomag Wheels*, designed to attract a new wave of fans to the brand.

Geomag has all the hallmarks of a classic toy, reaching out across a wide range of ages and appealing to our innate desire to build things, whether it be a simple cube, a car or a rhombicosidodecahedron. It should be around for a while yet.

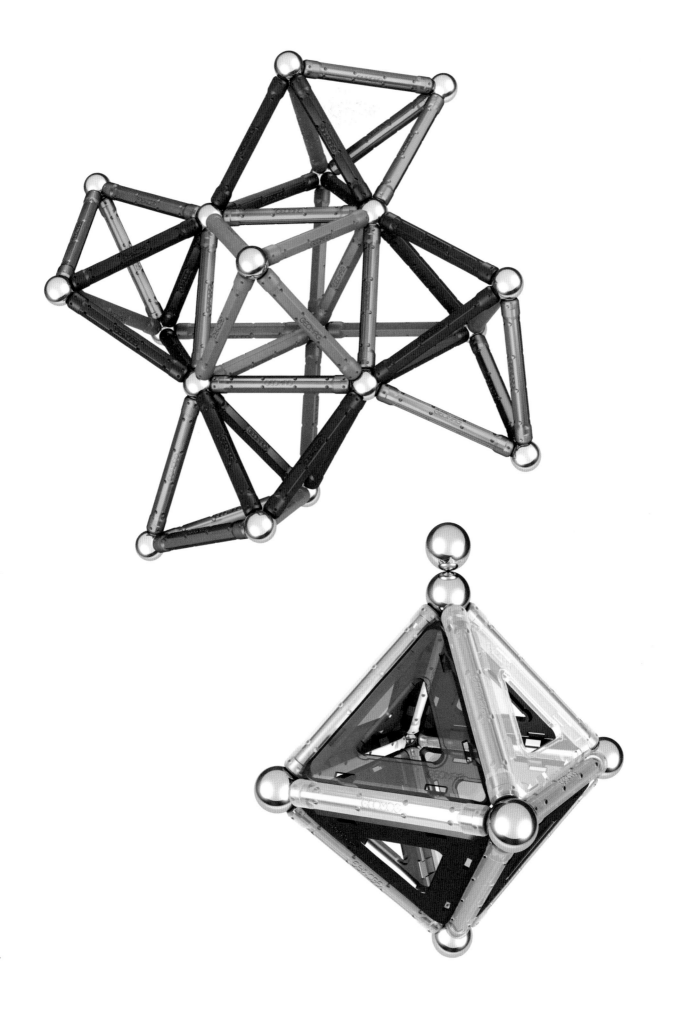

and finally...
THE CARDBOARD BOX

Every parent dreads buying their child an expensive toy, only to see the toy ignored after half an hour while the child clambers into the cardboard box it came in and plays happily for hours.

This nightmare scenario can easily be turned to the parent's advantage, by simply giving the child a few cardboard boxes to play with in the first place. The wonder of a child's imagination will do all the hard work and the boxes will quickly be transformed into something else entirely.

Calvin, from the Bill Watterson comic strip Calvin and Hobbes, is a perfect example. Turn his cardboard box one way and it is a 'transmogrifier', able to turn him into any creature he wants to be. Turn it the other way and it is a time machine, whisking him and his stuffed tiger, Hobbes, on any number of adventures.

Cardboard boxes can be painted and repainted. They can have bits cut out and stuck on. They can be joined together to form trains, houses or forts. They can become the body of a robot, the fuselage of a plane or the stages in a skyscraper. You can even easily add wheels to them with the release of Flair's new RoloBox.

It's the most versatile, most universally appealing and most creative toy that has ever been created. And it wasn't even designed to be a toy.

PICTURE CREDITS

Every effort has been made to credit the appropriate source. Please let us know if there are any omissions or errors and we will put them right in the next printing.

Cover: Bear (Merrythought); Barbie (Mattel); Mr. Potato Head (Hasbro); Meccano; Sylvanian Families (Flair); Buckaroo (Hasbro/David Smith); Rubik's Cube (John Adams); Marbles (David Smith); Scalextric; Space Hopper (Wow! Stuff). Alphabet blocks (Unclegoose).

Lindenwood Inc. (Uncle Goose) (10-11); Meccano (12-13); K'Nex (14, 198-199); Hasbro (15, 26 (Toy Story 3 Buckaroo!), 28-29, 46-47, 56, 66, 69 (Travel Mastermind), 84-85, 126-127, 128-129, 137 (Nerf Super Soaker), 138-139, 140-141, 147 (Jango Fett figure), 170-171, 182-183); LEGO (16-17); Stokys Systeme AG. (18-19); KAPLA (20-21); David Smith (22-23, 26-27, 31, 34-35, 38-39, 44-45, 49, 50-51, 52-53, 54-55, 57, 67, 68-69 (vintage Master Mind), p70-71, 89 (Stylophone Tune Book), 92-93, 100 (Bugs Bunny View-Master reels), 101, 122 (Sheriff and Indian figures), 130-131, 146-147, 154 (generic Army Man figure), 155, 156, 157 (Britains mortar crew, from the personal collection of Richard Fearnall), 183 (Play-Doh compound), 187 (Silly Putty), 192); Glenn Broadway (30); Nick Cooper (33); Mattel (36-37, p.59 (modern Rock 'em Sock 'em Robots), 112-113, 132-133, 149, 160-161, 162-163); Arthur Shemitz (40-41, 58-59 2001 Rock 'em Sock 'em Robots); Dan Hyer (41 (vintage Rebound box)); Rainbow Designs (42-43); Mark Rose (49); John Adams (48, 114-115, 188-189); icollector.com and Rich Penn Auction Company (59 original Rock 'em Sock 'em Robots); BRIO (60-61, 176-177); Inkwina (62 Subbuteo

Argentina figure); Sportingn (63 Vintage Subbuteo equipment); Laurent van Roy (63 1970s heavyweight Subbuteo players); GEOToys (64); Ravensburger (64-65); Eric Baetscher (74 tennis ball); Cliff Cheng (74 Adidas Jabulani football); Torsten Bolten (75 Wilson NFL football); Tage Olsin (75 baseball); Brookite (76-77); Charlie Brown image p.76 © Peanuts Worldwide LLC; Flair (78-79, 144-145, 186, 187 (Bionic Putty), 190-191, 193, 202-203); Early Learning Centre (80, 86, 136-137) Wham-O (80-81, 90-91, 94-95, 98-99); Radio Flyer (82-83); Catherine Yeulet (87); re:creation (88-89); H. Grossman Ltd (96); Parker Deen (97); Catherine Lane (100 red View-Master); Wow! Stuff (102-103 tandem space hopper has worldwide intellectual property); The Rocking Horse Shop (104-105); Character (106 Yomega Fireball yo-yo, 143); Wicked Vision (106-107); Raggedy-ann.com (110-111); Cabbagepatchkids.com (116-117);Le Toy Van (118); Playmobil (119, 122-123); Reeves International (120-121); Dolls House Emporium (124-125); Sideshow Collectibles (129 Duke 12in. figure); Schleich (134-135); Pkruger (136 water pistol boy); Tony Galla (142); Vivid (148); Margarete Steiff GmbH (150-151); Merrythought (152-153); Airfix (154-155 British Eighth Army box artwork and Aifrika Korps figures, 184-185); William Britain (157 Super Deetail figures); Jeff Thomas (160 Matchbox Models of Yesteryear B-Type Bus); Robinator (162 1969 Hot Wheels Twin Mill); Corgi (164 Land Rover and modern Aston Martin); Tooveys Antique & Fine Art Auctioneers & Valuers (164 vintage James Bond car); Tomy (165, 178-179); Little Tikes (166); Zeon Tech (167); Scalextric (168-169); Lionel Trains (172-173); Hornby 174-175; Automoblox (196-197); Thinkway Toys (200-201); Sean Locke (204); MBPHOTO (205);

This book is dedicated to my two boys, Harry and Joshua.

I am grateful for the assistance of many people while writing this book. In sourcing photographs I was helped greatly by Kate Adams and Flo Levy at Disney, Adrian Norman at Scalextric, Alison Kirkham at Character, Amanda Bick at Uncle Goose, Rupert Toovey & Co Ltd, Benn Bramwell and Sarah Stevens at Ravensburger, Vicki Douglas, Holly James and Jacey Bunker at Mattel, Charles Platt at raggedy-ann.com, Charles Williams and Chris Cotton at Wicked Vision, Laura Davis at Peanuts Worldwide LLC, Emma Owen and Melissa Wallace at LEGO, Kathleen Fallon at Reeves International, Fay and Ernst Schmid at Stokys, Gill Fountain at The Wagon Company, Heidi Bridges and Marissa Black at Sideshow Collectibles, Abi Hutchinson at Mothercare, icollector.com and Rich Penn Auction Company, Jane Cook at the Rocking Horse Shop, Jane Slatter at Amaze Marketing, Jeff Ball and Mandy Harrison at Brookite, Jo Haysom and Susan Journeaux at Flair, Joshua Toff at Zeon Ltd, Jude Kilama at Fosbury PR, Julie Pittilla at Pittilla PR, Laura Allen at Threepipe, Leyla Maniera at Steiff, Sarah Holmes at Merrythought, Tony Galla at Stretch Armstrong World, Louise Hathaway at Norton and Company, Louise Hatton at the Dolls House Emporium, Margaret McLean at Cabbage Patch Kids, Molliee Martin at Wham-O, Martyn Weaver at Corgi, Mary Captieux at re:creation, Matt Ashba at Lionel Trains, Michele Bates and Claire Taylor at Evolution PR, Nick Mouton at Mason Williams, Nina Sawetz at Bottle PR, Paul Maskew at Wow! Stuff, Renate Pooyé at KAPLA, Thierry Bourret at Asobi, Glenn Broadway, Nick Cooper, Kevin Wells, Arthur Shemitz, Dan Hyer and Richard Fearnall.

I would also like to thank my publisher, Lee Ripley, for all her help and support during the creation of this book, and Ray Watkins, of PriceWatkins, for her wonderful design work.

THE END

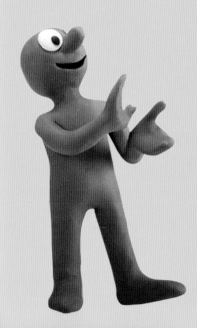